PRAISE FOR
Faith Begins at Home

Christian parents have a complex and stressful responsibility to pass faith on to their children. Mark Holmen gives families a language and the needed practical tools to communicate faith in Jesus to our children.

Rev. T. J. Anderson
Vice President, National Youth Events

Recent surveys of the evangelical Christian community by The Barna Group and *Newsweek/Beliefnet* indicate that our conservative, traditional theological views of the faith could be in jeopardy. I agree with Mark Holmen that it is critically important to teach our children a biblical worldview. The message in Mark's book stresses the importance of beginning this process in the home. My prayer as you read this book is that you and your children will be strengthened in your walk of faith.

Bob Creson
President, Wycliffe Bible Translators USA

Pastor Holmen connects personal story, family practice of faith and biblical plan and direction to the home. He challenges senior pastors and congregations to move into partnership with the home as the primary place to nurture faith! Parents and other adult caregivers will also find the practical applications in each chapter of this book to be a great tool for use with their families.

Dr. Dick Hardel
Author, *FaithTalk™ with Children* and *Blest Be the Pie That Binds*
Director, Vision and Creative Ministries
The Youth and Family Institute
Bloomington, Minnesota

Mark Holmen is passionate about the family and wants every home to do family God's way—not the world's way. His years of experience first as a youth and family minister and now as a senior pastor of a strong and rapidly growing congregation have given him incredible insights on the subject. *Faith Begins at Home* is packed full of good biblical teaching, family activities and small-group discussion ideas to help you in building strong families. I strongly recommend this book.

Dr. Bill Hossler
President, Missionary Church Inc.

With an alarming number of children leaving the Christian faith in their college and young adult years, it's time to reevaluate how we do church. It's time for the church to begin equipping parents—especially fathers—to bring up their children in the training and instruction of the Lord. Mark Holmen's book is a practical, balanced and fresh approach to family ministry that every church leader and Christian parent will want to read.

Rusty Russell
Director, Family Ministries
Southeast Christian Church, Louisville, Kentucky
Coauthor, *When God Builds a Church*

Brimming with biblically based common sense, Mark Holmen offers the modern family a model and practical steps on growing faith at home. I especially appreciated his strategy of a church-home partnership.

Tim Smith
Author and Speaker
President, Life Skills for American Families

FAITH BEGINS
AT HOME

Regal

From Gospel Light
Ventura, California, U.S.A.

MARK HOLMEN

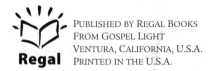

PUBLISHED BY REGAL BOOKS
FROM GOSPEL LIGHT
VENTURA, CALIFORNIA, U.S.A.
PRINTED IN THE U.S.A.

Regal Books is a ministry of Gospel Light, a Christian publisher dedicated to serving the
local church. We believe God's vision for Gospel Light is to provide church leaders with
biblical, user-friendly materials that will help them evangelize, disciple and minister to
children, youth and families.

It is our prayer that this Regal book will help you discover biblical truth for your own life
and help you meet the needs of others. May God richly bless you.

*For a free catalog of resources from Regal Books/Gospel Light, please call your Christian supplier or
contact us at* 1-800-4-GOSPEL *or* www.regalbooks.com.

Library of Congress Cataloging-in-Publication Data
Holmen, Mark.
 Faith begins at home / Mark Holmen.
   p. cm.
 ISBN 0-8307-3813-4 (trade paper)
 1. Family—Religious life. I. Title.
BV4526.3.H65 2005
248.4—dc22

2005025510

5   6   7   8   9   10   /   10   09   08

Rights for publishing this book in other languages are contracted by Gospel Light Worldwide, the international nonprofit ministry of Gospel Light. Gospel Light Worldwide also
provides publishing and technical assistance to international publishers dedicated to
producing Sunday School and Vacation Bible School curricula and books in the languages of the world. For additional information, visit www.gospellightworldwide.org;
write to Gospel Light Worldwide, P.O. Box 3875, Ventura, CA 93006; or send an e-mail
to info@gospellightworldwide.org.

Contents

Foreword

Mark Holmen is not the first person to write a book, even a Christian-oriented book, about family development and childrearing. Today when I "Googled" these terms, it appeared that there are well over 150,000 such books in print! Do we need to sacrifice one more forest for another such book?

In this case, I would enthusiastically answer yes! First of all, I have known Mark for years and have come to trust him as a man of God, a pastor, a Bible teacher and a friend. If he says he has something important to say about his area of expertise and passion, it is in my own best interests to pay attention. Second, I have witnessed his work with children and families and know that he is serious, competent and gifted in this arena. His years of experience and his passion for helping families, exhibited in ministry settings throughout the country, merit our consideration when he addresses this issue.

Consequently, it was with great anticipation that I read his manuscript on ministry to family. You see, Mark's family ministry was one of the models I studied most closely some years ago when I was conducting research about what makes a church's ministry to family most effective. During the writing of *Transforming Children Into Spiritual Champions*, I spent many months traveling the country, seeking to identify ministries anywhere in the nation that were effectively seeing children become all that God meant for them to be, and facilitating effective parenting as the key to that process. Mark's ministry was one of the most effective I found anywhere in the U.S. I learned a lot from him then, and I'm still learning from him today. This book is his most recent educational tool.

As you read these pages, you will encounter important parenting, family development and faith-building concepts. Each of those areas serves as a personal challenge to us: Have I really established my family as a top priority in my life? Can my kids understand and live a more faithful life by watching what I do? Have I truly devoted the necessary resources to making my family life as good as God wants it to be? Is my faith discernible by my lifestyle, not just through my passionate words regarding family life? What older adults, whose experience is priceless, am I learning from while I'm on this journey? What are my expectations of the local church in relationship to my efforts as a parent? These and other helpful questions emerge from the text as Mark pushes us to consider everything about our family life.

Theory is helpful, but the delivery of viable, practical suggestions is where the rubber meets the road for most parents. This book is full of rubber! It contains a dynamic blend of biblical insight, personal experience, research revelations and doable applications for those who love Christ and want their home to reflect His presence and His principles.

Once again, Mark Holmen has helped me—this time in my most important role, that of parent. Let his years of experience help you, too. Our God and your family will be blessed by it.

George Barna
Ventura, California
September 2005

ACKNOWLEDGMENTS

This book is dedicated to the memory of my father, Arlen

"Uncle Arlie" Holmen, who died on November 23, 2004.

My dad was my mentor, role model, friend and hero who,

together with my mom, Myrne, showed me how to

"do family right."

I also want to thank my wonderful wife, Maria,

and my daughter, Malyn, both of whom share my passion for

families. While their names may not appear on the cover,

their fingerprints are throughout this book. They are my primary

source of inspiration, support and understanding. Thank you

both for your unconditional love and willingness to be

transparent with our lives. I love you both.

Introduction
The Functional Dysfunctional Family

On October 31, 1995, at 12:13 A.M., my life changed forever. My wife, Maria, and I found ourselves in a birthing room at North Memorial Hospital in Minneapolis. We'd been married for five years, but we now stood at the brink of becoming parents for the first time. For three hours I steadfastly stood by Maria's side, serving as her focal point as she went through contraction after contraction.

Then the incredible moment of truth arrived! Our daughter, Malyn, came into the world. What an amazing sight to see! Immediately, the nurses whisked her away to the other side of the room to clean and measure her.

Malyn was crying loudly, but Maria was also groaning from the pain of delivering her first child. To this day I remember standing halfway between them wondering, *Which way do I go? Do I go to the side of my wife, who has just gone through one of the most exhausting and painful experiences of her life? Or do I go to the side of my precious little girl who is crying for the first time?*

Then the voice of God spoke to me—which, oddly, sounded a lot like Maria's voice—and commanded, "Go make sure Malyn is okay." My daughter had been in the world for just 60 seconds, and as a parent, I already needed help!

The Search for Success
Many parents today are searching for help. They want to succeed! They surf the Internet, watch Oprah and Dr. Phil, and buy every self-help book that comes out, all in an effort to keep their families together for another day. Yet families

seem to be hanging on by a thread. In our desperate search for answers, I wonder if we realize that God is there for us. He desires that our families not just survive, but also thrive as we journey through life!

Once I preached a sermon titled "The Functional Dysfunctional Family." I believe that every family is dysfunctional. In fact, in my 15 years of serving as a youth and family minister and as a senior pastor, I have yet to run into a family that claims to be perfect and in need of no help.

When I was growing up, my family was no different. On the surface we were a strong Christian family of five that included my parents and two older sisters. My dad was a camp director and my mom was an incredible person whom many called a living angel. A lot of people thought we were the perfect family. Yet little did they know that behind the scenes, my dad was a closet alcoholic.

I remember coming home many times to find my dad passed out in his recliner after drinking a series of martinis. I recall one time asking if my friend Danny could stay overnight and my mom answering no because dad was drunk again. I was so angry with my father that I went over to his recliner, looked him right in the eyes and said, "I hate you!" Although he was barely coherent, he groggily looked up at me and responded, "I hate you, too."

I'll always remember that evening. I'll always regret that evening, too. Thankfully, my dad kicked alcoholism a few years later and we went on to have many good years together. The point is that I come from a dysfunctional family. Yet God found a way to make us a functional dysfunctional family.

It was probably this upbringing that gave me the desire and passion to work with families. For 12 years, as I served three different churches as a youth and family pastor, I had the opportunity to travel across the country as a speaker and consultant.

Hardly a week would go by when I wasn't involved in some sort of family crisis or counseling situation. Often, I found my heart breaking for families. Yet I also had the opportunity to work with thousands of families who were succeeding, and I was able to watch and learn from them. From this vantage point, I've observed what works and what doesn't, and I look forward to sharing those insights with you in this book.

Where We're Headed

Let's take a quick look at what we'll explore together in the following chapters.

First, chapter 1 examines the status of families today, the makeover that needs to happen within each family, and the critical choice all families need to make if they want to succeed.

Chapter 2 gets personal with parents. In this chapter, I challenge parents to take an in-depth look at their own personal walk with the Lord and the role this plays in their families.

Chapter 3 focuses on our most precious commodity—our children—and what they need in order to succeed.

> Satan will do everything in his power to keep you from trusting God because he doesn't want you to discover the truth that God wants your family to thrive!

Chapter 4 helps families reestablish ways to use the gifts and experiences of grandparents, elders and mentors in our families.

Finally, chapter 5 examines the role the Church can and should play in the life of every family—as well as the role the Church shouldn't play in families.

Satan's Lie

I'm tired. In fact, I'm sick and tired of watching Satan strategically and methodically tear families apart. Satan loves to destroy families because he knows that the deep hurt and disillusion-ment this destruction causes can drive people away from God and the Church for generations. Many people don't trust God or have abandoned the Church because of something that took place in their family years ago.

Perhaps this describes your situation. If so, I want you to know that Satan is a liar. The Bible says that when Satan lies, "He speaks his native language, for he is a liar and the father of lies" (John 8:44). Satan will do everything in his power to keep you from trusting God because he doesn't want you to discover the truth that God wants your family to thrive!

God wants you, your children, your grandchildren and the many generations to follow you to live good long lives! The Bible says, "Live in deep reverence before GOD lifelong, observing all his rules and regulations that I'm commanding you, you and your children and your grandchildren, living good long lives" (Deut. 6:1, *THE MESSAGE*).

The Goal of This Book

While all families are dysfunctional, God loves families. He wants all families to be functional and succeed. The purpose of this book is to show you another way as a family. It's really pretty simple. As you bring Christ into the center of your home, you'll always have a way out of any situation Satan throws at your family. My goal is to provide biblical wisdom along with practical ideas that you can implement today to make your family—no matter how dysfunc-tional it seems to be—a functional family.

Regarding Biblical Wisdom. The Bible is a tried-and-tested book that can transform your family for the better. But you need to read what it has to say and then do what it tells you to do. The apostle James wrote, "Do not merely listen to the word, and so deceive yourselves. Do what it says. . . . The man who looks intently into the perfect law that gives freedom, and continues to do this, not forgetting what he has heard, but doing it—he will be blessed in what he does" (Jas. 1:22,25). The Bible contains what you need to succeed as a family because, as Hebrews 4:12 tells us, "The Word of God is living and active." It's not some out-of-date, out-of-touch book that has nothing to offer. The Bible has helped families for generations gone by and it will continue to help families for generations to come. The question becomes, Will you let the Bible help you?

Regarding Practical Ideas. I'm not a fan of books that simply point out problems but never spend any time providing solutions. Therefore, you will find a wealth of practical ideas in this book that you can begin implementing immediately to make over your family. My prayer is that the practical approach of this book will inspire, motivate and equip you to be the strong, healthy and joy-filled family that God intended you to be.

Other Things to Note

Before you read on, let me point out just a few of the elements you'll find at the end of each chapter that will help you get the most out of this book.

Makeover Keys. As I was writing, I was thinking of you. What I mean is that I tried to write without thinking about writing. Instead, I thought of myself having a casual, warm and meaningful conversation with a good friend. You know how those conversations go—you tell a story about yourself or another friend to emphasize a point you're making, share a Bible verse or a song that has been particularly meaningful to you, and express your disappointment or joy over events or situations. I do all of these things in these pages. However, because I also want to make sure that I'm absolutely clear about how you can make over each aspect of your family, I close each chapter with several "makeover keys." These statements summarize what you should take away from each chapter. And once you've read the whole book, they also provide a great "cheat sheet" to remind you what to work on in your family.

Family Activities. When I see something that works, I want to copy it. Like you, I want my family to succeed, and I'm not too proud to take an idea from another family and implement it in my own. Each chapter closes with family activities that have worked for other families, and these activities can also work for you. I can't stress enough how important these activities are. Of course, I encourage you to read the main body of each chapter. But jumping in and doing the activities in each chapter is where the real family makeover will take place. Some of these activities are fun, while others are more sobering and challenging. But each one will move you closer to being the kind of family you want to be—and more importantly, toward being the kind of family God wants you to be!

> The Bible has helped families for generations gone by and it will continue to help families for generations to come. Will you let it help you?

Small-Group Discussion Starters. Shortly after Malyn was born, Maria and I joined our first small group. The group consisted of four couples who all had children less than six months old. At first, none of us were sure if the group would be worth the time and effort, but we continued to meet. Over time, relationships grew and the small group became a place where we could share the highs and lows of trying to be a family in today's crazy world. Nine years have since passed, and many more children have come into the picture. The group has become a place where we simply "do life together." Even though Maria and I have moved from Minnesota to California, we still get together once or twice a year with this group because we truly don't know how we would get through life without the support of our closest friends.

When our group of fledgling families was just getting started, we would sometimes read and discuss a book together. My hope is that this will be a book that parents of both just-beginning and well-established families will discuss together. As a result, you will find some discussion-starter questions at the end of each chapter. If you're already in a small group, I think that you will find these helpful. If you're not in a small group, maybe this book will serve as a catalyst to help you start one.

So there you have it! In the chapters that follow, my prayer is that God will inspire, motivate, challenge and equip you to be the family that He wants you to be. It's not easy being a family today, yet with God's help we can all succeed because that is His plan and purpose for all families, no matter what shape or size they are. So let's begin our journey of allowing God to shape us and mold us into the family that He intends us to be. That journey begins in the home.

CHAPTER 1

The Home Makeover

I grew up living at a Bible camp. What a great place to live! I had a 500-acre backyard, horses, campfires, soccer fields and a hundred new friends to play with every week. If I didn't like my friends one week, I knew I'd get a hundred new ones the next week!

I always loved the skits the campers did—even the ones that I had seen over and over. While sometimes these skits were just silly and fun, I realize now that many of them had a very poignant spiritual point. One of my favorite camp skits was "Jesus Is Coming." The skit begins with a family sitting together at home when the phone rings. The caller is Jesus, and He notifies the family that He's coming over that evening. After determining that the phone call isn't a prank—because the phone had been disconnected two days earlier—the family realizes that they have to get ready for Jesus' visit.

They hastily begin cleaning up the house. The dad scrambles to replace pictures on the wall with crosses. The mom hides the magazines from the coffee table and puts out the Bible in their place. The teenage son discreetly removes some questionable items from under his bed. Other family members scurry to rid their house of all things "unholy."

During the frenzy of preparing for Jesus' visit, three separate visitors come to the door. The first visitor asks for donations for the local food bank. The second visitor says that he is raising money for a battered women's shelter. And the final visitor has just had a car accident and asks to use the phone to call for help. On all three occasions, the family rushes the visitor out the door, exclaiming, "We're too busy right now—a very important guest is coming! Go next door to the Smiths!"

The family looks at the clock. It's just one minute before midnight, so they know that Jesus will be coming any second. To really impress Him, they all sit down, open the Bible randomly and begin to read. The text that they happen to turn to is Matthew 25:41-45:

> Then he will say to those on his left, "Depart from me, you who are cursed, into the eternal fire prepared for the devil and his angels. For I was hungry and you gave me nothing to eat, I was thirsty and you gave me nothing to drink, I was a stranger and you did not invite me in, I needed clothes and you did not clothe me, I was sick and in prison and you did not look after me." They also will answer, "Lord, when did we see you hungry or thirsty or a stranger or needing clothes or sick or in prison, and did not help you?" He will reply, "I tell you the truth, whatever you did not do for one of the least of these, you did not do for me."

By the time the family is finished reading this passage, the hour has struck midnight. The teenage son says, "I guess Jesus isn't coming after all." After a moment of silence the mother responds, "I think Jesus was already here."

Reality Check

This skit has always been a reality check for me. It brings up all kinds of questions: What would I clean up around my house if Jesus were coming? How many times have I turned Jesus away from my home? Would I even realize that Jesus had been in my midst, or would I be too busy to notice? This skit can help us recognize an important truth: A makeover needs to happen in our homes.

Chances are you've seen those television shows in which a home is transformed right before your eyes in just a few days. Of course, I get drawn into the emotion and excitement that these physical changes bring to the family. But then I wonder, *Has this really helped the family?* While the makeover of the physical structure of a home is amazing, I believe that most families need a much deeper makeover—one that changes how they live, play and behave.

When I was a teenager, one Sunday my family had a huge fight in the car on the way to church. I have no clue what it was about, but I remember that we fought like cats and dogs all the way to church until we parked the car and walked toward the church doors. As we entered the church, the pastor greeted us and said, "How are the Holmens this fine day?" Instantly, we put on our Sunday smiles and responded, "Just fine!"

Now I look back and wish that our family had possessed the courage to look the pastor in the eye and say, "Not well at all. We need help!"

Many families today are like this. They find themselves in a cycle of unhealthy behavior, yet when asked how they're doing, they simply say, "We're fine!" And with artificial grins pasted on their faces, they keep going—yet deep down, they want to cry out for help.

Most parents today would like to raise a family at least as well or better than the way they were raised, but they need help. The first step in any recovery program is to admit that you need help. The day my daughter was born, I realized that I needed help. I know that I will need help every day on my family's journey through life, and I'm not afraid to admit it.

God's Way or the World's Way?

When it comes to a home makeover, you have a choice to make: Who will do the makeover? The choice you need to make is clearly spelled out in Joshua 24:14-15: "Now fear the LORD and serve him with all faithfulness. . . . But if serving the LORD seems undesirable to you, then choose for yourselves this day whom you will serve . . . But as for me and my household, we will serve the LORD."

Ultimately, the way your family functions—and whether it even survives—comes down to choosing whether you're going to do life God's way or the world's way. When Joshua admonished the people of God to make the choice, they answered, "Far be it from us to forsake the LORD to serve other gods! We too will serve the LORD, because he is our God" (Josh. 24:16,18). Joshua then challenged their sincerity by saying, "You are not able to serve the LORD. He is a holy God; he is a jealous God" (Josh. 24:19). But the people responded all the more adamantly, "No! We will serve the LORD!" (Josh. 24:21). Joshua then replied, "You are witnesses against yourselves that you have chosen to serve the LORD" (Josh. 24:22). Joshua was basically telling the people that he expected to see their lives reflect the choice that they had made.

While Joshua issued this challenge to the people of Israel in the Old Testament era, the same choice is ours to make today. Joshua said that the choice involves serving God with *all* faithfulness. Note that he didn't give the people an ancient version of "what happens in Vegas stays in Vegas." He didn't say that you could live a godly lifestyle at church and another lifestyle away from church.

What if Joshua had said to "serve the Lord with *some* faithfulness," allowing us to pick and choose when we want to do what God wants us to do? Wouldn't that be nice? To be honest, no, it wouldn't. God wants us to make a choice to serve Him with *all* faithfulness because anything else is sin. And sin hurts and destroys families. Affairs hurt spouses and children, divorce tears apart families, pornography destroys trust, violence leaves wounds for a lifetime. God knows that sin is destructive, and He has your family's best interest in mind when He asks you to serve Him with *all* faithfulness.

Of course, that won't always be easy.

I'll never forget when this issue hit home for my friend Jim. We'd been workout partners for about a year, and we usually met three times a week at our health club. One day I arrived before Jim and began to work out. When Jim arrived, he came up to me in his street clothes and said, "Mark, I can't work out today. But I need to talk to you." I could tell by the look on his face that something major had happened.

We went to the café and sat at a table together. Jim told me that his wife, Lisa, had just informed him that she had been having an affair for the past year. Jim was devastated. He and Lisa had been married for 10 years and they had two beautiful daughters under the age of eight. I'll never forget the look on his face when he asked me, "What am I supposed to do?"

This was a huge moment of truth for Jim. Lisa had confessed a sin and wanted forgiveness. She was open to whatever Jim decided, but she sincerely wanted to restore the relationship that had been strained for the last few years. I wish I could say I gave Jim the exact words he needed to hear that day. But to be honest, I don't remember a lot of what I said. What I do remember is that we cried together and prayed together, and then I challenged Jim to seek God's will before he made any decisions. The easy road for Jim was divorce. Yet as Jim searched God's heart, he knew divorce wasn't what God intended. He recognized that he hadn't been the perfect husband and had even contributed to Lisa's choices in some ways. Over the following weeks and months, Jim took the hard road and headed into counseling with his wife.

Fast forward 10 years. Jim called and asked if his family could come to California to stay with us for a spring break vacation. On a few occasions over the years, I'd had the opportunity to get together with Jim, but this would be the first time in 10 years that I'd see his entire family together. I remember at one point during their visit, I watched as Jim and Lisa sat together in an overstuffed chair, laughing and smiling with their children (now two teenagers and a new addition who is five). Watching this family share a joy-filled time together brought me to tears. God had restored the relationship, and their family was strong because Jim and Lisa made a choice to serve the Lord with *all* faithfulness. The world had offered them another choice, and some friends had encouraged them to make that choice. But even in the most difficult of times, Jim and Lisa had trusted that God could do something in their relationship. And God did.

What's Your Choice?

Has your family made the choice to serve God in all faithfulness? Are you "all in" as a family for God? Is your family living in a way that reflects the commitment you've made?

I think that many of the problems families face today are a direct reflection of the less-than-all commitment they've made to the Lord. Many families "play Christians" on Sunday mornings, but they don't want to "be Christians" the rest of the week. And then they wonder why things aren't going well.

As families, we need to echo Joshua's declaration: "As for me and my household we will serve the Lord!" We have to go after it 100 percent. This means choosing to do life God's way. It means allowing Him to make over our families. He has our best interest in mind: "'For I know the plans I have for you,' declares the LORD, 'plans to prosper you and not to harm you, plans to give you hope and a future'" (Jer. 29:11). That sounds like a pretty good promise to me! God wants our families to flourish. He wants to give us hope and a secure future.

Moses wrote, "See, I am setting before you today a blessing and a curse—the blessing if you obey the commands of the LORD your God that I am giving you today [to love the Lord your God, to walk in all His ways and to hold fast to Him]; the curse if you disobey the commands of the LORD your God and turn from the way that I command you today by following other gods, which you have not known" (Deut. 11:26-28). This is by far the most important choice you'll ever make. God wants to bless you and your family. But you need to choose to follow Him with all faithfulness. Failing to do so leads to all sorts of problems in families, and many of us know the mess these problems cause.

God Sees Past Your Mess

When I entered into family ministry, I quickly learned that it's a messy business. Dealing with families, you face everything from divorce to clinical depression to teenaged rebellion to every kind of addiction imaginable. I had parents tell me, "You don't want to hear about the issues we have as a family." But none of that matters to God. He's not intimidated by your messy situation.

And His offer to make over your family isn't a one-time-only offer. You can choose to follow Him wholeheartedly today no matter what choice you've made in the past. The choice you make has eternal ramifications.

I vividly recall sitting in a board meeting at church the day after Easter. As I was in the middle of my report, a cell phone rang. The board member quickly turned down the ringer and left the room to answer the call. When he came back just a few moments later, he had tears in his eyes. "That was my wife," he said. "Brian just called. His two sons were in an accident. Kenny [age 7] was killed instantly and Zachary [age 5] is in intensive care."

Brian and his wife, Lili, were a faithful family who clearly lived a life with Christ at the center. Brian had three older children from a previous marriage, and he and Lili had brought two wonderful boys into the world, Kenny and Zachary. We immediately ended the meeting, and three of us headed to Brian and Lili's home. On the way, we learned more of the details. The boys had been with their uncle, aunts and cousins at Disneyland. As they were leaving the park, a vehicle ran a red light and collided into them as they were walking across the crosswalk.

> God is not intimidated by your messy situation. And His offer to make over your family isn't a one-time-only offer.

The hours seemed like days and the days like weeks as we prayed for Zachary's recovery. At the same time, we had to plan a funeral for Kenny. Brian and Lili were devastated.

I spent hours in prayer asking the Lord to give me something to say to the family during the funeral. What follows is a portion of what I shared with them during that difficult hour.

The most predominant question people, including me, ask at a time like this is, Why, Lord? As I searched through Scripture, I discovered that when it comes to hard times like this, there's no complete answer. In 1 Corinthians 13:12, Paul writes, "Now we see but a poor reflection . . . then we shall see face to face. Now I know in part; then I shall know fully, even as I am fully known." This simply means that one day we'll understand. But not today.

While we can't fully understand, we can see that God's hand is resting upon you as a family. God came into each of your lives. Both of you chose to follow Him. When you married, you invited Christ to be in the center of your family life. As a result, you parented Kenny in a manner that led him to invite Jesus into his heart. You're truly a Deuteronomy 6 family—you love the Lord with all your heart, soul and strength. And you passed this love for the Lord on to your children. Kenny declared his commitment to the Lord at an early age because you loved the Lord. Kenny loved the Lord so much that he made you get up and come to the 6:30 A.M. Easter sunrise service, because he wanted to go to church on Easter before going to Disneyland.

I'm at a loss for what to say to your family today. What I do feel compelled to say is simply, "Aren't you glad you made the choice to make Christ the center of your home?" Because of your choice, Kenny chose to give his life to Christ at a young age. As difficult as this day is, I can't imagine what it would be like if you hadn't chosen to follow Christ. In the midst of your pain and mourning, you can have peace and assurance knowing that Kenny is in heaven today and that his death is not the end of his life, but just the beginning.

So I want to ask one more time, What's your choice? It doesn't matter what your answer was in the past. Today you can make a new choice. Your family's makeover can start today.

The apostle Paul said, "Therefore, if anyone is in Christ, he is a new creation; the old has gone, the new has come!" (2 Cor. 5:17). This can be the description of your family if you simply choose to be an "all in" family. It will be a choice that you will never regret.

Home Makeover Keys

Key 1: Realize that your family needs a makeover. The first step in any recovery program is to admit that you have a problem. All families have problems and can benefit from a makeover.

Key 2: Choose the best makeover specialist. Don't settle for second best when it comes to your family. The world offers many makeover specialists with all sorts of ideas. But they pale in comparison to the Lord, the only One who can truly make all things new in your family.

Key 3: Be patient. Makeovers are messy. The changes that need to take place in your family may create a mess. Give God time.

Key 4: Remember that the end result is worth it. If you allow God to make over your family, the result will be far better than you could ever imagine.

Family Activities

ACTIVITY 1
Blessing Your Home[1]

Remember Joshua's personal declaration when he challenged the people to be all in for God? He said, "As for me and my household, we will serve the LORD!" (Josh. 24:15).

You and your family can use the following service of blessing to make the same declaration. Invite friends, family and your pastor. Two or more people—including you, your spouse and your pastor—can share the leadership roles marked "Leader 1" and "Leader 2."

Involve your children and their friends as much as possible. Have younger kids lead the procession from room to room in follow-the-leader style. Older children (and other adults) can take turns reading some of the Scripture verses marked "Reader."

Gather your entire group together, either outside the home or in the garage. If you gather in the garage, use only the candle for your light to make the Scripture reading more meaningful. Take the lighted candle from room to room as a symbol of the light of Christ coming into each room of the house. You may want to use a large candle that can remain in a prominent place in your home after this time of blessing.

1. In the Garage

Leader 1: We welcome all of you to this special service of blessing in which we will boldly proclaim that "as for me and my household, we will serve the LORD" (Josh. 24:15). We recognize that "every good and perfect gift is from above" (Jas. 1:17), and it is for this reason that we have gathered here today. Our home and our family are gifts from God, and we want to establish this home as the primary place where our faith will be nurtured. This home is a place where we will laugh together and cry together. We will pray together. And we will grow in our faith together here.

Reader: Proverbs 24:3-4 says, "By wisdom a house is built, and through understanding it is established; through knowledge its rooms are filled with rare and beautiful treasures."

Reader: Matthew 5:14-16 reminds us, "You are the light of the world. A city on a hill cannot be hid. Neither do people light a lamp and put it under a bowl. Instead they put it on its stand, and it gives light to everyone in the house. In the same way, let your light shine before men, that they may see your good deeds and praise your Father in heaven."

Leader 2: God, just as this candle gives light to this home, enable those who live here to be Your light in the world. Grant them Your wisdom and understanding. In Jesus' name, amen.

2. At the Entrance of the Home

(Encourage the young children to lead the procession from the garage to the entrance, while the rest of the group plays follow the leader.)

Leader 1: Many people will come and go through this entrance. In Revelation 3:20, Jesus says, "Here I am! I stand at the door and knock. If anyone hears my voice and opens the door, I will come in and eat with him, and he with me." Today we open these doors and say, "Come into our home, Lord Jesus!"

Reader: Psalm 121:8 says, "The LORD will watch over your coming and going both now and forevermore."

Leader 2: Lord Jesus, we welcome You into this home. Protect and guide those who live here, their going out and their coming in. Let them share the hospitality of this home with all who visit, that all who enter here will know Your love and peace. In Jesus' name, amen.

3. In the Living Room/Family Room

Leader 1: Family and friends will gather in this room. We'll laugh here and relax. This will become a soft place to land after a hard day, and it will be a place where we will have many meaningful conversations.

Reader: John 13:34-35 says, "A new command I give you: Love one another. As I have loved you, so you must love one another. By this all men will know that you are my disciples, if you love one another."

Leader 2: God, bless all who gather in this room. Bless their conversations. Guide and direct what they watch on TV. Knit them together in Your love and fellowship. In Jesus' name, amen.

4. In the Study or Library

Leader 1: As the family uses this room to read books, do homework, run a business, use the computer and make important decisions, we ask the Lord to guide and direct everything that happens here.

Reader: Proverbs 9:9 says, "Instruct a wise man and he will be wiser still; teach a righteous man and he will add to his learning."

Leader 2: God, You are the teacher who leads us to all truth.

Grant that those who study and learn here may use the knowledge that You give to accomplish the purpose and plan You have for their lives. In Your name, Lord Jesus, we pray, amen.

5. In the Kitchen

(Have a plate of cookies waiting.)

Leader 1: This will probably be the busiest room in the home, as the family prepares meals and guests participate in great conversations. Something about the kitchen draws people together. God knew that much of our lives would revolve around food, and in the Scriptures He used food to teach us important truths.

Reader: In 1 Timothy 6:8 Paul writes, "But if we have food and clothing, we will be content with that."

Reader: In Matthew 6:25, Jesus states, "Therefore I tell you, do not worry about your life, what you will eat or drink; or about your body, what you will wear. Is not life more important than food, and the body more important than clothes?"

Reader: In John 6:27, Jesus says, "Do not work for food that spoils, but for food that endures to eternal life, which the Son of Man will give you."

Reader: Proverbs 25:21 says, "If your enemy is hungry, give him food to eat; if he is thirsty, give him water to drink."

Leader 2: God, help us to be hungry for the right things in life. Bless all the conversations that will take place in this room and send Your blessing upon those who work in this kitchen. Remind us to be thankful for our daily provision. In Jesus' name, amen.

6. In the Dining Room

(Have the younger children lead the group as you hold hands and form a circle around the dining room table.)

Leader 1: As families get busier, dining rooms seem to be used less and less. Yet when Jesus wanted to have an intimate moment with His disciples, He gathered them together for a meal, where He would break bread with them. This room will serve as a place where Jesus can gather your family together to have intimate moments with family and friends.

Reader: Zephaniah 3:20 reads, "At that time I will gather you; at that time I will bring you home."

Leader 2: Blessed are You, Lord of heaven and Earth, for You work in ways that we can't see. Gather us together around this table and bless the time we'll spend here. Draw us closer to one another and to You through the conversations that will take place here. In Jesus' name, amen.

7. In the Bedrooms

(Let the younger children run ahead and play Hide and Seek.)

Leader 1: Each day concludes in these rooms. At times we'll come into the bedroom exhausted, and other times we'll struggle to sleep due to the excitement of the coming day. In these bedrooms, we'll also have many private times of prayer and reflection. Here we'll have some of our most intimate times with each other and with God.

Reader: Hebrews 10:21-22 reads, "Since we have a great priest over the house of God, let us draw near to God with a sincere heart in full assurance of faith."

Reader: In Psalm 4:8, we read, "I lie down and sleep in peace, for you alone, O LORD, make me dwell in safety."

Leader 2: Guide us waking, Lord, and guard us sleeping, that awake we may walk with Christ and asleep we may rest in Your peace. In Jesus' name, amen.

8. In the Guest Room
(Have you found the kids who are hiding yet?)

Leader 1: Friends and family will visit and stay in this room. We look forward with anticipation to the guests that we will have the opportunity to host and welcome into our home.

Reader: In Romans 15:7, Paul writes, "Welcome and receive [to your hearts] one another, then, even as Christ has welcomed and received you, for the glory of God" (*AMP*).

Leader 2: God, refresh all who visit here, and during their time in this home, may they feel Your overwhelming presence so that they may know Your grace and love. In Jesus' name, amen.

9. Back in the Living Room
Leader 1: We've now come back to where we started. Before we conclude this service of blessing, let's hear from God's Word about the reason we're here.

Reader: From Joshua 24:14-15: "Now fear the LORD and serve him with all faithfulness. Throw away the gods your forefathers worshiped beyond the River and in Egypt, and serve the LORD. But if serving the LORD seems undesirable to you, then choose for yourselves this day whom you will serve . . . but as for me and my household, we will serve the LORD."

Leader 2: God, we thank You for this home and welcome You into our home. We don't want You standing outside at the door knocking. We want You in the center of our life as a family, and we thank You for the way You've provided for our every need. We dedicate this home to You. We pray that all we do in this place will bring You glory and praise. In Jesus' name, we pray, amen.

Note
   1. Reprinted and adapted from *Occasional Services,* copyright © 1982. Used by permission of Augsburg Fortress.

ACTIVITY 2
WWJHMD in the Home?

In the late 1980s, a Christian bracelet became incredibly popular and well-known throughout the world. Woven into the simple bracelet were the letters "WWJD." These letters stood for "What Would Jesus Do?" People wore the bracelet to remind themselves to live as Jesus would live.

While I loved what the bracelet stood for, I always thought two additional letters were needed. If the bracelet read "WWJHMD," it would stand for "What Would Jesus Have Me Do?" The difference is significant. We can say, "What would Jesus do with my in-laws?" yet this doesn't involve us much at all. But if we were to say, "What would Jesus have *me* do with my in-laws?" it completely changes things. Now we have to do something. The question becomes, "Am I going to do what Jesus asks me to do?"

As a family, use markers and different-sized Post-it Notes to create WWJHMD reminders. Pretend you're hiding eggs for an Easter egg hunt and place the WWJHMD Post-It Notes throughout your house. Take some of them to work and to school, and don't forget to put one in each car that you and your family own.

ACTIVITY 3
Family Mission Statement

Another good way to start your family makeover is by writing a family mission statement to guide and direct you as a family of faith. My wife, Maria, and I wrote our family mission statement a few years ago as we were driving to Iowa. We had this mission statement engraved onto a wood plaque that we display on our living room wall. Here is our family mission statement:

The Holmen family

We are a Christian family who:

1. *Unconditionally loves, supports, nurtures and forgives each other.*
2. *Demonstrates fiscal responsibility, including giving of our time, talents and treasure to the Lord.*
3. *Models faith through what we think, say and do.*

Use the following process to come up with your own family mission statement:

1. As parents, talk about the nonnegotiable things that you want the mission statement to convey. A good question to help you get started is, If someone described your family to another person, what would you like them to say about you?
2. Discuss these nonnegotiable values with your children. Make sure they completely understand and support these values.
3. Guide your family to create a mission statement that matches these agreed-upon values. While you want to involve your kids in this process, remember that

you're the parents and must take the lead. God has given you the responsibility to lead your family because you have wisdom, experience and a larger perspective than your children.

4. When the mission statement is complete, involve your younger children by working together to make a family mission statement banner or poster. Proudly display your mission statement in a prominent place in your home.

Small-Group Discussion Starters

1. If a complete stranger visited your home, based on what he or she sees, what would that individual say you worship?
2. If Jesus came to visit and stayed at your home tomorrow, what changes would you make? What prevents you from making those changes today?
3. If you could make over one thing in your family today, what would that be?
4. Have you faced a difficult choice about whether to keep your family together? Are you and your family facing a challenge right now to serve the Lord with *all* faithfulness?
5. Would you say that you are "all in" as a family for God? Is your family living life in a way that reflects the commitment you have made?

The Parent Makeover

The phone rang in my office at church. It was Alan Thompson, an active member of the congregation. While he often chatted with me at church, he rarely called. I presumed something was wrong.

He stammered a bit, searching for the right words. "I'm having troubles with my 15-year-old, Andrea," he said.

"What do you mean by troubles?" I asked.

"We're not communicating very well, and it seems like we're always on opposite ends of every situation. I'd like to talk with you to see if there is anything I can do so that we're not always fighting."

Realizing that Alan needed more than a quick answer over the phone, I went over to his home. Alan, his wife and two children lived in a beautiful home. By the world's standards, they appeared to have everything together. Alan was involved in a variety of committees at church, and his wife helped out with Sunday School. His daughter, Andrea, was actively involved in the youth ministry, and she also helped teach Sunday School.

When I arrived, Alan and I sat down in the living room. For the first 30 minutes, he shared story after story of how disrespectful Andrea had become. "She doesn't listen to me anymore," he said. "And whenever I establish a rule or guideline, she always seems to push just beyond the limit, which forces me to have to do something about it. I'm also concerned about the friends she's hanging out with, and I'm wondering if I need to limit how much time she can spend with them."

As Alan continued ticking off his concerns, I remember thinking to myself, *What am I going to say? I don't have a teenager and I've never had to face this myself.* When Alan had finally exhausted himself of stories related to his daughter's behavior problems, he turned to me and asked, "What am I supposed to do?"

Not wanting to let on that I felt ill equipped to handle his family's situation, I did what I always try to do when I get in over my head. I turned to God for help. Then I sat back in the chair, turned to Alan, and said, "Have you prayed with Andrea about this?"

This didn't seem like an outrageous question to me. I'd seen Alan lead prayer many times at committee meetings, and his daughter led prayer in Sunday School every week. Yet the look in his eyes told me all I needed to know.

Over the first 15 years of Andrea's life, Alan had been actively involved in taking her to daycare, soccer practice, piano lessons and even church. But he had never prayed with his daughter. And the idea of praying with her for the first time as a teenager seemed utterly beyond the scope of reason.

What Are You Passing On?

Alan Thompson's experience is the reality in many Christian families today. We may go to church, but we don't bring home the most important thing we need: faith!

One of my favorite songs has the following chorus:

Have we taught our children well,
is our life a show and tell,
can they see the love of Jesus in our eyes?
And when another page has turned,
do you think they will have learned,
to show the love of Jesus with their lives?
Have we taught our children well?[1]

As parents, we pass on things to our children every day. They're watching us, learning from us and emulating us. The question is not *are* we passing things on to our children, but *what* are we passing on to our children. I'm proud to have taught my daughter how to swing a golf club, shoot a basketball and ride a bike. But I'm not so proud that I've taught her how to get frustrated with slow drivers and red lights. And she's only nine!

> The question is not *are* we passing things on to our children, but *what* are we passing on to our children.

While teachers and coaches play a significant role in teaching our kids how to read, write, have good manners, participate in sports and play musical instruments, any teacher or coach will tell you that parents play the primary role in reinforcing that instruction in the home.

In my early years as a youth and family pastor, I was satisfied if I had a lot of teenagers involved in the youth ministry. I thought

I was doing my job if I reached teens for Christ and took them on youth trips and to Bible camp. One day, I received a questionnaire to give to the teenagers in my youth group. It was titled "The Most Significant Religious Influences" survey, a national survey conducted by the Search Institute to help determine what factors influenced teens in their faith.[2]

I strategically gave the questionnaire to my students after we'd been on a youth trip together, figuring this would increase my score. As instructed, I collected the surveys and sent them in. It took months to get the results, but I still remember receiving the envelope stamped with the words "Survey Results Inside." I was on my way to a youth board meeting and I thought this would be the opportunity of a lifetime. I was certain that the results would show that I, the esteemed youth and family pastor, was the top influence in the faith journey of our church's youth. I even wondered if these results would strengthen my case for a raise.

At the meeting, I opened the letter and began to read the results. According to the survey, the most significant religious influence for Christian teens today is . . . Mom.

At first I was upset, but then I quickly rationalized that no one can compete with moms. So I moved on. The second most significant religious influence for Christian teens today is . . . Dad.

This one hurt. I'd been around most of these teenagers' dads, and I knew that I spent more time with their kids than they did! How could dads possibly be more influential than I was?

My heart continued to sink as I read that significant religious influence number three was a grandparent, followed by friends and siblings. "Youth group leader at my church" was way down the list. At that point, I accepted the reality that parents are the primary influences in the faith development of children—and that a lot of people topped youth pastors.

Chart 1 Mainline Protestant Youth Most Significant Religious Influences[*3]

MOST SIGNIFICANT RELIGIOUS INFLUENCES	Percent Choosing as One of Top 5							
	GRADE						GENDER	
	7th	8th	9th	10th	11th	12th	M	F
Mother	87	75	77	72	75	75	81	74
Father	64	51	55	49	57	51	61	50
Grandparent	36	28	29	34	27	22	30	29
Another relative	11	12	14	16	12	7	13	12
Siblings	22	14	13	13	15	14	18	14
Friends	22	24	28	25	31	31	22	29
Pastor	60	56	49	45	36	49	57	44
Church camp	23	30	26	25	23	23	20	28
Movie/music star	3	3	4	4	2	2	4	3
Christian Education at my church	23	30	25	25	31	25	26	26
Church school teacher	29	27	17	23	20	23	26	21
Youth Group at my church	25	25	32	33	33	34	30	30
Youth Group Leader at my church	13	11	20	17	17	15	15	16
Youth Group outside my church	3	6	2	3	4	5	4	4
Youth Group Leader outside my church	2	1	1	3	4	4	2	3
The Bible	25	30	27	23	16	26	24	25
Other books I have read	2	3	4	4	3	4	3	4
Prayer of meditation	9	15	15	16	20	18	11	19
School teacher	3	5	2	2	3	6	3	4
Revivals or rallies	3	3	4	4	5	4	3	4
TV or radio evangelist	2	·	1	·	·	·	1	1
Worship services at church	10	10	10	16	14	15	12	13
God in my life	3	3	11	11	13	13	8	13
Work camp	·	1	4	2	5	5	3	3
Mission study tour	0	0	·	0	1	1	·	·
Retreats	7	12	16	20	17	18	11	17
Coach	2	2	3	3	4	4	4	2
Choir or music at church	11	12	8	9	11	6	7	12

*Includes mainline Protestant youth only (CC, ELCA, PCUSA, UCC, UMC) weighted by congregational and denomination size.

As a youth and family pastor, this was hard to admit. After all, I was trained in how to put together youth trips, lead youth music and direct a great Sunday School program where *we* taught faith to the children. But no one had trained me to equip the *parents* to pass on the faith to *their* children. Marjorie Thompson, director of the Pathways Center for Christian Spirituality, echoes what I was learning firsthand: "For all their specialized training, church professionals realize that if a child is not receiving basic Christian nurture in the home, even the best teachers and curriculum will have minimal impact. Once-a-week exposure simply cannot compete with daily experience where personal formation is concerned."[4]

As researcher George Barna notes, "When a church—intentionally or not—assumes a family's responsibilities in the arena of spiritually nurturing children, it fosters an unhealthy dependence upon the church to relieve the family of its biblical responsibility."[5] Martin Luther put it this way: "Most certainly father and mother are apostles, bishops, and priests to their children, for it is they who make them acquainted with the gospel."[6] And above all, Scripture is clear that it is the parent's responsibility and honored privilege to pass on the faith to their children (see Deut. 6:6-7). Your home is a church!

Living, Breathing Disciples

A while back, I was speaking to a group of parents and teenagers. I began the talk by having them respond to a series of statements.

"Raise your hand if you can name one of the twelve disciples." Nearly every hand in the room went up.

"Raise your hand if you could name a living disciple today." About half of the hands went up.

"Raise your hand if you believe in Jesus Christ as your Lord and Savior." Again, every hand went up.

I then told the teenagers and parents to look at each other as I made the following statement: "Realize that the person you are looking at, someone who stated that he or she believes in Jesus Christ as Lord and Savior, is a disciple of Jesus Christ."

The crowd began to murmur a little, and then from the front row a young man pointed his finger at his dad and loudly proclaimed, "No way! Not him!" The young man then tried to go on to tell me all the ways that his dad was not a disciple of Christ!

Obviously, this wasn't the point of the exercise. But it did make a powerful point. Our children are watching us to see if our behaviors reflect the faith we proclaim.

Whose Job Is This?

Many parents today would rather pass on the responsibility of being the "bishops, apostles and priests" to the "professionals" at church instead of modeling those roles themselves. But why?

One reason why parents won't take the lead when it comes to discipling their kids is because they didn't experience what it was like to have Christ as a part of the home that they grew up in. This was the case with Alan Thompson. It's not that he didn't want to pray with his daughter; it's just that no one had ever shown him how. Many parents stray simply because they know no other way.

However, the more prevalent reason why parents have passed to the Church the responsibility of teaching their children faith is because the Church has enabled them to do so. In the 1960s and 1970s, the Church saw an explosion in Christian education through Sunday School and youth group ministries. Churches added education wings and youth rooms to their facilities. At the same time, society entered into the technology age and families began to get busier. Work schedules increased and more moms started working. When the church began offering ministries for children and teenagers, parents welcomed the opportunity to bring their kids to church for a time of Christian education and fun. Quite honestly, for many parents, this provided a needed break from their children.

While everyone's intentions were good, many parents started to see these programs as an opportunity to pass on the faith-nurturing responsibilities to the church. Parents dropped off their kids and said, "Here you go. Teach my children faith. I'll be back in an hour to pick them up."

Of course, the church never intended for these programs to take the place of parents in the faith development of children. However, intentional or not, over the last 30 to 40 years, there has been movement away from the home being the primary place where faith is nurtured. Researcher George Barna notes, "A majority of churches are actually guilty of perpetuating an unhealthy and unbiblical process wherein the church usurps the role of the family and creates an unfortunate sometimes exclusive dependency upon the church for a child's spiritual nourishment."[7]

While the approach of "dropping off the kids at church" might keep them busy at church for a few years, it often doesn't lead to faith that lasts into their adult years. At a conference I attended, national youth ministry specialist Dawson McAlister stated, "Ninety percent of kids active in high school youth groups do not go to church by the time they are sophomores in college. One third will never return."[8] I believe that the reason these kids don't return to church is because faith hasn't been firmly established and lived out in their homes. In fact, many of them view faith as something hypocritical—parents act one way at church and a completely different way at home. When the teenagers become young adults, they simply conclude, "If that's what Christianity is about, I don't want anything to do with it."

Faith Starts with You

If we want our children to have a faith that influences the way they live their lives—and the critical life decisions they make—then in our homes we need to be modeling faith through a personal relationship with Jesus Christ.

Deuteronomy 6:4-6 says, "Hear, O Israel: The LORD our God, the LORD is one. Love the LORD your God with all your heart and with all your soul and with all your strength. These commandments that I give you today are to be upon your hearts."

Moses is speaking to families in these verses, letting us in on the key to succeed as a family. As you reread the verses above, notice the word that's repeated the most. *Your* God, *your* heart, *your* soul, *your* strength. The key is recognizing that *you* have one God—Father, Son and Holy Spirit—who wonderfully and uniquely made you in His image. But He didn't just create you. This God loves you so much that He saw you in your fallen state, destined to spend eternity in hell, so He sent His one and only Son to die for you so that you can have a new life filled with peace, hope and assurance. You and your family's success begins with *you* and your willingness to let Him into your life and the very core of your family.

> If we want our children to have a faith that influences the way they live their lives, then in our homes we need to be modeling faith through a personal relationship with Jesus Christ.

I once led a workshop with David Anderson titled "Nurturing Faith of Teenagers." I set the stage for the workshop by helping the parents identify the characteristics of teenagers as well as the issues they commonly face today. Dr. Anderson then took it a step further by asking the parents, "How many of you wish your teenager had a stronger faith?" Every hand in the room went up. He then made a comment that I'll never forget. He said, "While it's good that everyone desires that our teenagers have a stronger faith, the truth is that what we see in our teenagers' faith is a mirror image of our own faith. So, the issue is not their faith, but your faith."

This leads us to an important question: Where is Christ standing in your life? Is He at the very center of your life, influencing the decisions you make and the way you live your life? Or is He still outside knocking?

The answer to this question is so important because it directly relates to your family. I know you want what's best for your family. In fact, I'm convinced that parents today are committed to doing a better job at parenting and to having a stronger family than the ones they were raised in. Youth and family pastor Mark DeVries writes, "In my fifteen years of youth ministry, I have never seen parents more hungry for help than they are now. They want to spend more time with their children. They feel acutely the need to be better equipped as parents."[9] Well, here's your chance! It begins by opening the door and letting Jesus into your life and into your home.

I remember once seeing a copy of a great painting by Raphael titled *Jesus at the Door*. The painting depicts Jesus standing at a door knocking. A vine winds around the doorway, and it looks as if the door hasn't been opened for some time. I heard that when Raphael first showed the painting, a critic pointed out that he had forgotten to paint a handle on the door. The painter replied that he didn't forget; the handle was just on the other side of the door.

We have a God who stands knocking at the door of our hearts. He has always been there, and He waits there until we let Him in. "Here I am! I stand at the door and knock. If anyone hears my voice and opens the door, I will come in and eat with him, and he with me" (Rev. 3:20). God is waiting for you to invite Him to help your family. He has what your family needs to get you through the good times and the bad. He can rebuild relationships, heal wounds and bring hope to the most hopeless of situations. He won't barge into your life. Yet He will persistently and patiently stand at the door of your life, knocking and waiting to be invited in.

Here's my point: The makeover in your family begins with a makeover in your own heart. If you want your children to have a personal relationship with Christ, you need to have a personal relationship with Christ. If you want God to make over your family, the makeover must begin with you. You need to move from having knowledge about God in your head to establishing a personal relationship with God in your heart. Only then can God affect how you live your life, raise your children, and make life decisions.

There's an old saying that the distance between your head and your heart is only about six inches, but it's the most difficult six inches that anyone can travel. However, I think the path between the head and the heart is where life gets exciting. That's why I want to explore how you can move your faith from your head to your heart using a slightly unconventional analogy—my experience with whitewater rafting.

The Ride of Your Life

If you've never gone whitewater rafting, I can tell you that it's exciting, stimulating, completely life changing and utterly terrifying! When you arrive at a whitewater rafting base, you are loaded into buses and taken slowly up switchback roads to the entry point. Because the roads overlook the river, for the seemingly endless journey up the mountain, you're confronted with the reality of the huge rocks, steep falls, fast moving rapids and hairpin turns that you will soon be attempting to raft over. As you look at the rushing river, you continually think to yourself, *What have I gotten myself into? Isn't there another way? Can I really make it?*

These are thoughts and fears that afflict many parents today. How many times have you found yourself saying, "What have I gotten myself into? Isn't there another way? Can I really make it?" Every parent today has fears. Yet God knows your fears, and He has provided everything you need to make this journey.

A Map of the River: The Bible. One of the ways I got past my initial fears of whitewater rafting was to realize that others had taken the same journey before me and survived. After our group got off the bus, we saw pictures and videos of other groups that had successfully made it down the river. A huge map on the wall continually updated the condition of the river and the locations of dangerous areas. Just by looking at the map, the pictures and the videos of those who had rafted before me, I instantly felt my confidence increase.

In much the same way, the Bible is full of examples of people who have gone before you—examples that you can learn from. The Bible serves as a reliable map to guide you down the river of life. The more you read it, the more aware you'll be about trouble areas and what you need to do to avoid or get through them. Psalm 119:105 puts it simply: "Your word is a lamp to my feet and a light for my path."

Satan doesn't want you to read the Bible, because he realizes that this will make the journey of faith easier for you. He will do his best to keep you so busy that you won't be able to spend time in God's Word, for he knows that the Bible will be of no help to you if you don't read it, trust it and follow it. The apostle James wrote, "Do not merely listen to the word, and so deceive yourselves. Do what it says" (Jas. 1:22).

The Guide: Jesus Christ and the Holy Spirit. After we watched the video of previous groups and studied the map of the river, we were introduced to our raft guide. Nothing made me feel more secure than when our guide said he had been a guide for more than 15 years and had made the trip down the river more than 200 times. Talk about a confidence booster! I was also relieved when our guide said, "I'll be getting in the boat with you, leading you down the river myself." I wouldn't have been too excited if he'd said, "Good luck, hope you make it!" But our guide was right in the boat with us, directing us at every turn. He shouted instructions to us, helped us through dangerous situations, encouraged us when we were down and celebrated victories with us.

> If you truly trust God in your heart, you will listen to His voice and do what He says.

Scripture says that God provides a guide for your life—His only Son, Jesus Christ—to show you the way through life and to eternity. In John 14:6, Jesus said, "I am the way the truth and the life. No one comes to the Father except through me." All you need to do is follow Him. God also provides the Holy Spirit, who will dwell within you and guide you each day. The apostle John wrote, "But the Counselor, the Holy Spirit, whom the Father will send in my name, will teach you all things and will remind you of everything I have said to you" (14:26). "When he, the Spirit of truth, comes, he will guide you into all truth" (16:13).

The Holy Spirit wants to serve as your personal OnStar life navigational system—available to you 24 hours a day, 7 days a week—to guide you through the ups and downs of life. Isaiah 30:21 says, "Whether you turn to the right or to the left, your ears will hear a voice behind you, saying, 'This is the way; walk in it.'" If you truly trust God in your heart, you will listen to His voice and do what He says.

The Raft: The Church. The rafts that we used, made specifically for whitewater rafting, were designed to help our group get down the river safely. However, when I first saw the raft that we would be using, my reaction was, "That thing is supposed to take us safely down the river?" The raft was old, worn out and covered with multiple patches. I wasn't certain that this boat could do the job. Yet despite its appearance, the raft helped us traverse the river safely. It provided far more protection than we ever thought that it would or could.

"Old, worn out, and covered with patches" are the words that some people use to describe the local church. Sometimes the local church seems outdated and in dire need of repair. When you add to this the reality that the local church is filled with sinners, no wonder people say, "How is that supposed to help me?"

Yet in spite of its imperfections and flaws, the Church is God's ordained Body. He created the Church to help you through the highs and lows that life will throw at you. "Just as each of us has one body with many members, and these members do not all have the same function, so in Christ we who are many form one body, and each member belongs to all the others" (Rom. 12:4-5).

Are you devoted in your heart to the Church? Are you in a committed relationship with the Bride of Christ, the Christian Church? Or are you just "doing church" because you think you're supposed to? We'll look more closely at how the Church can be involved in your family makeover in chapter 5.

The Crew: Doing Life Deeply Groups. I had a map of the river, my guide, and a raft. Just one thing was missing—the rest of the crew. As the other rafters began to gather and get into the raft, I thought to myself, *This must be a joke! These people clearly have no idea what they are doing, and this motley-looking crew has absolutely no chance of getting down the river safely. We're all going to die!* Of course, I was wrong. We worked well together under the direction of our guide. In fact, my crew even had to pull me out of the water when

I fell out of the raft. As they pulled me back into the raft, I was thinking, *I'm sure glad they couldn't hear my thoughts earlier!*

In the Introduction, I mentioned that Maria and I took a risk nine years ago and joined a couples' small group in our church. Joining a group of people that we didn't know was a real stretch for us. Nine years later, this group is like family to us, even though we're separated by more than 2,000 miles. We've laughed together and cried together. We've been through job losses, cancer, family crises, depression and relocations together. We've learned how to parent together and we've learned how to bring God into the center of our homes together. When we started, we had no idea what we were doing. But now we wouldn't know how to do life without each other.

God doesn't intend for you and your family to go through life alone. Hebrews 10:25 says, "Let us not give up meeting together, as some are in the habit of doing, but let us encourage one another." John 13:34-35 stresses how to encourage each other: "A new command I give you: Love one another. As I have loved you, so you must love one another. By this all [people] will know that you are my disciples, if you love one another."

Jesus' ministry began by calling together 12 disciples to "do life." Through this group, these men moved from knowing about Jesus in their heads to truly knowing Him in their hearts—even to the point of being willing to give their lives for Him. If you truly want to grow in your faith, I urge you to find a group of fellow followers to "do life" with.

If your church doesn't offer a small-group ministry, find two or three other people or couples in the same life stage that you are in. Ask if they would be willing to participate in a small group with you, meeting weekly or monthly for the purpose of growing stronger as a family. You might say something such as, "I don't know about you, but I sure find it hard being a family today. I'd like to get together with some other families who face some of the same issues and challenges my family is facing so that we can learn from each other. Would you consider meeting with us?"

The Ride: Life Journey. My raft trip down the river included all sorts of experiences. At times, the ride was smooth and easy and we relaxed and enjoyed the views. Other times, we were in the midst of fast-moving rapids, paddling for our lives! We also had some frightening moments when we wondered if we would make it. More than once, we were tempted to give up and abandon ship. Yet through it all we persevered. And when the journey was done, we looked back on the experience and said, "That was the ride of our life!"

Similarly, the ride through life for families today can be a very frightening and difficult ride. While you'll experience times when things go smoothly and easily, you'll also run into many rapids and rocks along the way. At times, you'll be tempted to give up. But if you have an unwavering faith and commitment to the Lord deep in your heart, you and your family can one day look back on this journey through life and say, "That was the ride of our life!"

Notes

1. Brent Henderson, "Have We Taught Our Children Well," Copyright ©1991 Discovery House Music/Knotty Pine Music (ASCAP). Used by Permission.
2. Search Institute is a nonprofit, nonsectarian research and educational organization that advances the well being and positive development of children and youth through applied research, evaluation, consultation, training and the development of publications and practical resources for educators, youth-serving professionals, parents, community leaders and policy makers. Phone: 1-800-888-7828. Website: www.search-institute.org.
3. Reprinted with permission from *Effective Christian Education: A National Study of Protestant Congregations.* Copyright © 1990 by Search Institute SM. Used by Permission of Search Institute. No other use is permitted without prior permission from Search Institute, 615 First Avenue NE, Minneapolis, MN 55413; www.search-institute.org.

4. Marjorie Thompson, *Family: The Forming Center,* rev. ed. (Nashville, TN: Upper Room Books, 1996), back cover.

5. George Barna, *Transforming Children Into Spiritual Champions* (Ventura, CA: Regal Books, 2003), p. 81.

6. Martin Luther, "The Estate of Marriage, 1522," quoted in Walther Brand, ed., *Luther's Works* (Philadelphia, PA: Fortress Press, 1962), p. 46.

7. Barna, *Transforming Children*, p. 81.

8. Dawson McAlister, *Finding Hope for Your Home* (Irving, Texas: Shepherd Ministries, 1996), n.p.

9. Mark DeVries, *Family-Based Youth Ministry* (Downers Grove, IL: Inter Varsity Press, 1994), back cover.

Parent Makeover Keys

Key 1: Mothers and fathers are the top two influences in the faith development of children. As a parent, you wield more than twice as much influence as any church program or ministry.

Key 2: Your child's faith will likely be a reflection of your faith. If you want your children to have faith that lasts, they need to see that your faith relationship with Christ is a lasting one.

Key 3: God provides you with everything you need to have a strong and growing faith: the Bible, Jesus, the Holy Spirit, the Church and fellow believers.

Key 4: Christ offers you the ride of your life. Will you take it? The decision you make will not only affect you, but your children and their children as well.

Family Activities

ACTIVITY 1 (FOR PARENTS ONLY*)
Inviting Jesus into Your Life

My prayer is that after reading this chapter, you will recognize the importance of inviting Christ to be at the very center of your life. If you have not already done so, I want to offer you the opportunity to invite Jesus to take up permanent residence in your life.

He's knocking, but He won't force His way into your life. You can simply open the door and invite Him in by sincerely and honestly praying the following prayer:

> *Dear Jesus, I recognize that You are God and that You have been standing at the door of my heart. You've been waiting patiently for me to open up my life to You. I'm sorry that I have left You standing out there for so long. I've been living according to the ways of the world, but now I want to live my life Your way. I open the door of my life to You. Jesus, come into my life as my Savior. You have promised that You will guide us and show us the best way to live for You when we invite You to be at the center of our lives. So I pray that You will guide my life and my family life as well. In Jesus' name, amen.*

---

* While most of the family activities are to be completed together as a family, these first two activities are designed just for parents. (If you have teenagers, they may want to participate in Activity 2.)

If you just prayed this prayer for yourself, this marks a new beginning for you and your family. Life will never be the same again! With Jesus in your life, you will have the opportunity to learn from Him, just as your children learn from you. His passion will become your passion and His power will become your power. You're going to learn to love what He loves—just as my daughter learned to love pepperoni pizza with salt on it, just like her daddy! This is just the beginning of a transformational work that God wants to do in your life and in the life of your family.

Get ready for the ride of your life!

ACTIVITY 2 (FOR PARENTS ONLY)
Personal Assessment

Take some time to assess where you are in your personal faith journey. Read through the following list and place a checkmark next to any statements that describe what's already going on in your life. Place a star next to those you want to start. Do this assessment individually, and then discuss your answers with your spouse.

❑ I'm reading the Bible and gaining encouragement from those who have gone before me.

❑ I'm turning to Jesus Christ and praying for the Holy Spirit to guide and direct me through life.

❑ I've jumped in and committed to a Christian church. I recognize that while the church has flaws, it is still what I need to get through this journey.

❑ I've found a crew of fellow believers to take the journey with me.

❑ I'm on the journey and find myself:

_____ at a smooth and easy place

_____ feeling scared as I hear the rushing waters ahead

_____ in the middle of some rushing rapids

_____ staring at a big rock that I have to hit head-on

_____ coming out of some scary rapids

_____ being tempted by Satan to give up

_____ nearing the end of my journey—and ready to do it all over again!

ACTIVITY 3
The Way I See Christ in You

Gather your family around the kitchen table and then give a sheet of paper and a marker to each member of your family. Instruct each member of your family to write the following sentence at the top of the paper:

"The way I see Christ in _____ [person's own name] is . . ."

For example, on my paper I would write, "The way I see Christ in Mark is . . ." When everyone is ready, have each family member pass his or her paper to the person on his or her left. Give everyone 60 seconds to write down whatever comes to mind to complete the sentence. When the 60 seconds are up, pass the papers to the left again, and continue doing so until everyone receives his or her own page back. Then go around the table and have each person read what the other family members wrote.

Activity 4
The Passion of the Christ

Today, we live some 2,000 years after Christ's ministry on Earth. Most of us find it hard to remain close to something that happened two years ago, much less 2,000 years ago.

The movie *The Passion of the Christ* gave us a very accurate and graphic depiction of what Christ did for us. The response to this movie was overwhelming. In my church, we sold out five private showings. I watched how this movie moved many people from head faith (knowledge) to heart faith (personal and committed) as it brought them face-to-face with the reality of what Christ willingly did for them. One person said to me, "I never realized how distant I'd become from Christ until I saw this movie."

Be warned that this isn't an easy movie to watch. I encourage you to watch the movie as a family, but I don't recommend it for children under the age of 12. Even the reedited version released in 2005 retains some very graphic footage.

Following the movie, read John chapter 20 for the rest of Jesus' story. As a family, talk about what parts of the movie affected you most. If the movie raises questions you can't answer, write them down and invite your pastor to meet with your family to discuss those issues.

Small-Group Discussion Starters

1. What is your greatest fear? What is your greatest desire?

2. What are some of the things you've passed on to your children? What behaviors and attitudes do you see in your kids that reflect your behaviors and attitudes?

3. In this chapter, I quoted Dr. David Anderson's statement that "what we see in our teenagers' faith is a mirror image of our faith." If your child's faith ends up becoming a mirror image of your faith, how will that make you feel? Would you describe your faith as a mirror image of your parent's faith?

4. Where are you in your personal walk with Christ? Is Jesus outside knocking, or have you let Him into your life? Is your faith more in the head or in the heart?

5. Go through Activity 2 and discuss your personal assessments with another member of the small group. In what areas are you progressing? In what areas do you need to make a start?

CHAPTER 3

The Child Makeover

If you have teenagers—or have even been to a mall recently—you probably already know that teens have tastes in music that differ significantly from yours.

One Christian dad I know, Rob, was becoming concerned about the music his teenage son was listening to. His son, Nick, was beginning to wear black T-shirts with band names on the front, and Rob saw an ever-growing collection of black-covered CDs in Nick's room with lyrics that he knew weren't healthy. But instead of just taking the CDs away, Rob tried a different approach.

On the way to school one day, he asked Nick, "What type of music do you like to listen to?" Nick answered that it was a combination of rap and heavy metal. Then Rob asked, "Could I hear two of your favorite songs?"

Nick, thinking he'd get into trouble, replied, "You wouldn't like it."

Rob persisted and said, "I promise you won't get in trouble. I just want to hear what your kind of music sounds like."

Nick reluctantly put a CD into the car's player, and Rob listened to two songs that made his hair—what he had left of it—stand on end. But he never made a comment. After the two songs were over, he simply said, "Thanks for letting me into your music world."

While Nick was at school that day, Rob went to a large Christian bookstore. He approached the employee working in the music section and said, "I need you to help me find the four best Christian hard rock and rap CDs that you have." The clerk was a little surprised by this middle-aged man's request, but she obliged.

Rob sat down at one of the store's listening stations and listened to each of the CDs. He purchased two that sounded similar to what he'd heard in the car. When he picked Nick up from school, Rob said, "Would you mind if I play you a couple of CDs I picked up today?"

Nick rolled his eyes and said, "Are you kidding?"

"Come on," Rob persisted, "I listened to your music. Just listen to these songs and tell me what you think." Nick reluctantly agreed.

When Rob turned on the first song, with the volume cranked up loud, Nick couldn't believe what he was hearing. "What's this?" he said.

"Just something I picked up that I thought you might enjoy," Rob replied. He went on to explain that he wanted Nick to have the freedom to listen to the style of music that he liked, but at the same time he was concerned with some of the lyrics and behavior of the groups that Nick was listening to. "One way to think about it," Rob said, "is to think about whether you'd feel comfortable reading the lyrics of your current CDs to me or our pastor." Rob told Nick that there were quite a few Christian groups who played the same type of music and that he just wanted to make Nick aware of it.

That evening, Rob and Nick went to the Christian bookstore and picked out eight additional CDs that Nick liked. Rob gladly paid the hefty price for the CDs. Nick now plays in a Christian rock band, and while Rob still doesn't care for the style of music Nick likes, he loves the message that Nick is getting.

This dad took a small—but significant—step in the makeover process of his son's life. As parents, we're in the child makeover business. If you haven't realized that yet, you will! As George Barna writes, "If you connect with children today, effectively teaching them biblical principles and foundations from the start, then you will see the fruit of that effort blossom for decades to come."[1]

> As parents, we're in the child makeover business. If you haven't realized that yet, you will!

How Will Your Child Turn Out?

I was at the grocery store recently, patiently standing in the checkout line. Suddenly, to my right, a child burst into a raging temper tantrum. I watched as the embarrassed mom tried to deal with her child. But the mother eventually gave up and just let the child throw his fit. My eye was then drawn to another checkout line where a mother stood with her two children who were about the same age as the boy throwing the tantrum. But these kids were simply standing, laughing and smiling as they patiently waited their turn. Instantly, I began to wonder, *How is my child going to turn out?* And more importantly, *What can I do about it?*

I think every parent wants the best for his or her children. We all want our kids to avoid drugs, alcohol, violence, gangs and promiscuous sexual activity. We want them to get good grades and maintain a healthy lifestyle. Yet we wonder how we can lead them to make good choices.

One person who had a great impact on my life, both as a youth and family pastor and as a parent, was Merton Strommen. Mert, the founder of Search Institute, was a research scientist who cared deeply about children.[2] One day, he pondered a simple question: Why do some children turn out well, while others don't? Of course, there's no simple answer to this question. So Mert put his research team to work. After collecting and evaluating mountains of research, the team identified 30 developmental assets (a list that has now grown to 40) that every child needs to succeed. These assets are defined as "concrete, common sense, positive experiences and qualities essential to raising successful young people."[3]

Chart 2

Forty Developmental Assets[4]

Search Institute has identified the following building blocks of healthy development that helps young people grow up healthy, caring and responsible.

EXTERNAL ASSETS

Category	Asset Name and Definition
SUPPORT	1. **Family Support**—Family life provides high levels of love and support.
	2. **Positive family communication**—Young person and her or his parent(s) communicate positively, and young person is willing to seek advice and counsel from parent(s).
	3. **Other adult relationships**—Young person receives support from three or more nonparent adults.
	4. **Caring neighborhood**—Young person experiences caring neighbors.
	5. **Caring school climate**—School provides a caring, encouraging environment.
	6. **Parent involvement in schooling**—Parent(s) is actively involved in helping young person succeed in school.
EMPOWERMENT	7. **Community values youth**—Young person perceives that adults in the community value youth.
	8. **Youth as resources**—Young people are given useful roles in the community.
	9. **Service to others**—Young person serves in the community one hour or more per week.
	10. **Safety**—Young person feels safe at home, at school, and in the neighborhood.
BOUNDARIES AND EXPECTATIONS	11. **Family boundaries**—Family has clear rules and consequences and monitors young people's behavior.
	12. **School boundaries**—School provides clear rules and consequences.
	13. **Neighborhood boundaries**—Neighbors take responsibility for monitoring young people's behavior.
	14. **Adult role models**—Parent(s) and other adults model positive, responsible behavior.
	15. **Positive peer influence**—Young person's best friends model responsible behavior.
	16. **High expectations**—Both parent(s) and teachers encourage the young person to do well.
CONSTRUCTIVE	17. **Creative activities**—Young person spends three or more hours per week in lessons or practice in music, theatre or other arts.
	18. **Youth programs**—Young person spends three or more hours per week in sports, clubs, or organizations at school and/or in the community.
	19. **Religious community**—Young person spends one or more hours per week in activities in a religious institution.
	20. **Time at home**—Young person is out with friends "with nothing special to do" two or fewer nights per week.

Chart 2 continued

INTERNAL ASSETS

Category	Asset Name and Definition
COMMITMENT TO LEARNING	21. **Achievement motivation**—Young person is motivated to do well in school. 22. **School engagement**—Young person is actively engaged in learning. 23. **Homework**—Young person reports doing at least one hour of homework every school day. 24. **Bonding at school**—Young person cares about her or his school. 25. **Reading for pleasure**—Young person reads for pleasure three or more hours per week.
POSITIVE VALUES	26. **Caring**—Young person places high value on helping other people. 27. **Equality and social justice**—Young person places high value on promoting equality and reducing hunger and poverty. 28. **Integrity**—Young person acts on convictions and stands up for her or his beliefs. 29. **Honesty**—Young person "tells the truth even when it is not easy." 30. **Responsibility**—Young person accepts and takes personal responsibility. 31. **Restraint**—Young person believes it is important not to be sexually active or to use alcohol or other drugs.
SOCIAL COMPETENCIES	32. **Planning and decision-making**—Young person knows how to plan ahead and make choices. 33. **Interpersonal competence**—Young person has empathy, sensitivity, and friendship skills. 34. **Cultural competence**—Young person has knowledge of and comfort with people of different cultural, racial or ethnic backgrounds. 35. **Resistance skills**—Young person can resist negative peer pressure and dangerous situations. 36. **Peaceful conflict resolution**—Young person seeks to resolve conflict nonviolently.
POSITIVE IDENTITY	37. **Personal power**—Young person feels he or she has control over "things that happen to me." 38. **Self-esteem**—Young person reports having a high self-esteem. 39. **Sense of purpose**—Young person reports that "my life has a purpose." 40. **Positive view of personal future**—Young person is optimistic about her or his personal future.

What made the research so eye-opening was the finding that nurturing assets have tremendous potential for reducing the likelihood that our kids will get into trouble down the road. The research revealed that the more assets children have in their lives, the less likely they are to become involved in at-risk behaviors like illicit drugs, alcohol use, early sexual activity, violence and so forth.

Chart 3   Assets in Relation to At-Risk Behaviors[5]

PROBLEM ALCOHOL USE	ILLICIT DRUG USE	SEXUAL ACTIVITY	VIOLENCE
(Three or more uses in the last month or got drunk one or more times in past two weeks.)	(Three or more uses in the past year.)	(Sexual intercourse, three or more times, lifetime.)	(Three or more acts of fighting, hitting, injuring a person, or using a weapon in the past year.)
If 0-10 Assets 49%	If 0-10 Assets 39%	If 0-10 Assets 32%	If 0-10 Assets 61%
If 11-20 Assets 27%	If 11-20 Assets 18%	If 11-20 Assets 21%	If 11-20 Assets 38%
If 21-25 Assets 11%	If 21-25 Assets 6%	If 21-25 Assets 11%	If 21-25 Assets 19%
If 26-30 Assets 3%	If 26-30 Assets <1%	If 26-30 Assets 3%	If 26-30 Assets 7%

Note: Finding based on surveys of over 217,000 sixth- to twelfth-grade youth in 318 communities and 33 states during the 1999-2000 school year. The same kind of impact is evident with many other problem behaviors, including tobacco use, depression and attempted suicide, antisocial behavior, school problems, driving and alcohol, and gambling.

In addition to protecting youth from negative behaviors, having more assets increases the chances that young people will have positive attitudes and behaviors, as the following charts show.

Chart 4   Assets in Relation to Positive Attitudes and Behaviors[6]

SUCCEEDS IN SCHOOL	EXHIBITS LEADERSHIP	MAINTAINS GOOD HEALTH	VALUES DIVERSITY
(Mostly As in school)			
If 0-10 Assets 8%	If 0-10 Assets 50%	If 0-10 Assets 26%	If 0-10 Assets 36%
If 11-20 Assets 17%	If 11-20 Assets 65%	If 11-20 Assets 47%	If 11-20 Assets 57%
If 21-25 Assets 30%	If 21-25 Assets 77%	If 21-25 Assets 69%	If 21-25 Assets 74%
If 26-30 Assets 47%	If 26-30 Assets 85%	If 26-30 Assets 89%	If 26-30 Assets 88%

Note: Findings based on surveys of over 217,000 sixth- to twelfth-grade youth in 318 communities and 33 states during the 1999-2000 school year.

The research gets even more interesting. Search Institute originally presented the 30 developmental assets randomly—with no levels of priority. In other words, the fifth asset on the list was just as important as the twenty-fifth. Yet Mert believed that one asset in particular on the list might have more value than the others. As I write this book, Search Institute is still conducting additional research to confirm the relationship between this one asset and the other assets. But early findings strongly indicate that this single asset is directly linked to at least 25 of the assets.

Would you like to know what one asset has the ability to provide your child with at least 25 of the other assets? It's the asset titled "Religious Community." Further, in a personal conversation I had with Mert, he stated that the term "Religious Community" has more to do with a personal faith relationship than with any established religion.

So let me summarize. We want our children to do well and avoid risky behaviors. The Search Institute discovered that if your child possesses 25 or more assets, there is an increased likelihood that your child will do well and avoid at-risk behaviors. A further study reveals that a personal faith relationship can instill at least 25 other assets into your children. Therefore, if you want what's best for your child, you can safely conclude that a personal faith is the most important thing that a child needs in his or her life. The question now becomes, How do we pass on faith to our children?

A Faith That Sticks

In chapter 2, we discovered that the primary way faith gets passed on to our children is through us—Mom and Dad. Now let's look at *how* we can do that. Let's start by returning to Deuteronomy 6.

> Impress them [the commands of the Bible] on your chil-
> dren. Talk about them when you sit at home and when
> you walk along the road, when you lie down and when

you get up. The LORD commanded us to obey all these decrees and to fear the LORD our God, so that we might always prosper and be kept alive, as is the case today (Deut. 6:7,24).

The word "impress" refers to a faith that sticks. It means constantly showing and instilling in your children an unwavering faith that will be with them their entire lives. Notice that these verses do not say to bring your children to Sunday School, drop them off at the front door, pick them up an hour later and "presto" they'll have faith. In fact, after 15 years in ministry, I can assure you that no matter how good the Sunday School or youth ministry is at your church, if you're not modeling, discussing and sharing your faith with your children in your home, their faith will most likely not stick when they grow older.

Eddie was a perfect example of this. He was involved in every youth program we had. He came to every youth night, attended every retreat and summer camp that we offered, and even became a leader in our youth program. Yet we never saw his parents except when they picked him up or dropped him off at church. At one retreat, when I asked him about his parents, he said, "They don't believe in Jesus, but they think church is a safe place for me to hang out. So that's why they let me stay involved in church."

When Eddie graduated from high school, he didn't have the money to attend college. So he worked. For a while, he stayed around church to help out with the youth program. But gradually, we saw less and less of Eddie. About 18 months after graduating from high school, Eddie was picked up for drunk driving. And that was just the beginning of a series of problems that Eddie would have.

Eddie hasn't set foot in church for years. It makes me wonder how a leader of a church youth group—someone who clearly demonstrated a strong personal faith in Christ—could end up abandoning the faith and end up in jail just a few years later. I believe the answer is that Eddie's faith was never firmly "impressed" on and in him. His faith wasn't grounded at home. Instead, other values were "impressed" on Eddie. His dad was an alcoholic and began to buy Eddie alcohol after his high school graduation, even though Eddie was underage. And Eddie's mom didn't really care if he continued going to church or not. Due to the influences that Eddie received in his home, faith looked like a program rather than a lifestyle to him. And when the program was done, so was Eddie.

If we want to make over our children with a faith that we impress on their hearts, we simply need to follow the instruction of Moses in Deuteronomy 6. It doesn't sound so difficult. These verses simply say to talk about faith with your children—to make "faith-talk" a part of your everyday vocabulary.

Are Parents Doing the Work?

Sadly, statistics show that when it comes to impressing faith on our children through faith-talk, we have some serious work to do. Search Institute conducted a nationwide survey of more than 11,000 participants from 561 congregations across 6 different denominations. The results were revealing:

- What percentage of teenagers have a regular dialog with their mother on faith/life issues? 12%
- What percentage of teens have a regular dialog with their father on faith/life issues? 5%
- What percentage of teenagers have experienced regular reading of the Bible and devotions in the home? 9%
- What percentage of youth have experienced a service-oriented event with a parent as an action of faith? 12%[7]

Researcher George Barna confirmed these numbers in his research for the book *Transforming Children Into Spiritual Champions.* "We discovered that in a typical week, fewer than 10 percent of parents who regularly attend church with their kids read the Bible together, pray together (other than at meal times) or participate in an act of service as a family unit. Even fewer families— 1 out of every 20—have any type of worship experience together with their kids, other than while they are at church during a typical month."[8]

> Faith is not something that can be taught; faith is something that must be caught.

When we recall that Mom and Dad are the top two influences on a child's faith, these statistics become even more sobering—and sad when you realize that the answer is pretty simple. As a parent, you need to be talking about and living out your faith with your children. That's it. If you remember nothing else from this book, please remember this old saying: *Faith is not something that can be taught; faith is something that must be caught.*

Catching faith is like catching a cold. When your child catches a cold at school and brings it into your home, what happens? The whole family eventually catches the cold! That's how it is with faith. If faith is in the home, everyone catches it! Faith-talk needs to be a part of everyday life—not just an hour a week on Sunday mornings.

Finding opportunities to talk about faith is not as difficult as it might sound. When Malyn was three years old, she went through a period in which she continually asked "why" questions. "Daddy, why is the sky blue? Why is grass green? Why is water wet?" I could have tried to answer her questions with scientific logic: "Well, the sky is blue because around the earth is a layer called the ozone, and the ozone is . . ." Instead, I used the opportunity to talk with her about God. "Malyn, the sky is blue because you have a wonderful

God who made that blue sky just for you. And God gave those white puffy clouds a special design that only you can see. Tell me what that cloud looks like to you . . . and grass is green because God knew you loved to slide on your knees and make green streaks on your blue jeans! And water is wet because God knew you'd love to play and swim, so he made it wet just for you to enjoy!"

When Moses stated that you should talk about your faith "when you lie down and when you get up" (Exod. 6:7), he meant all the time. Everything you go through on a day-to-day basis provides an opportunity to talk about faith and to teach your children to walk with the Lord. The key to faith-talk does not lie in having all the answers—the key is having the conversations! In these conversations you can "train a child in the way he should go, and when he is old he will not turn from it" (Prov. 22:6).

Take the T.R.A.I.N. to Faith-Talk

When it comes to knowing how to faith-talk with their children, many parents need help because they didn't experience faith-talk while they were growing up. One of my mentors, Roland Martinson, noted at a Youth and Family Institute conference, "The church's role is to be equippers of families. What we ought to do is let the children drop their parents off at church, train the parents and send them back into their mission field—their homes—to grow Christians."[9]

I like the idea of training parents. So I'm going to take Proverbs 22:6 one step further and "train the parents to talk with their children about faith, so when they are old they will not turn from it." Using the word "train," let's take a look at how you can use faith-talk to pass on your faith to your children.

T—Time

In today's world, time is one of our most precious commodities. The primary question I hear from parents is, "When is there time to talk with my child about faith?" For most parents, the stereo-typical image that comes to mind when you say "faith-talk" is having an hour-long, sit-down discussion at the kitchen table with the Bible open and a candle burning. Of course, the reality today is that a lot of families don't even have a kitchen table, and they certainly don't have a full hour when they can talk together!

In our increasingly busy lives, we must make the best of the time that we have. So when is the best time to discuss our faith with our children? The only reasonable answer is *anytime.*

In the Industrial Age, most people in America worked around the schedule of the factories—Monday through Friday, 9 A.M. to 5 P.M. Families had weekends and evenings free to spend with their kids. But in today's Quantum Age, many families find it difficult to establish the kind of routine that people had in the Industrial Age. This is a crisis—but it's also an opportunity.

Dr. Martinson has identified seven opportunities for nurturing faith in today's Quantum Age. Let's look at how we can use these opportunities to talk about faith with our children.

1. **Car Time.** Doesn't it seem that the most time you spend together as a family is when you're in the car, on your way to the next thing you have to do? Try turning off the radio and asking your children what "highs" and "lows" they had during the day. Then take a moment to pray for the event that you're headed to next.

2. **Sick Time.** Another significant block of time that you have with your children occurs when they are sick and have to stay home from school. While no one looks forward to his or her child being sick, it does provide time to have a healthy conversation. Sick time gives you a chance to watch videos or listen to music together. So why not choose videos that will naturally lead to talking about issues of faith and life?

3. **Bed Time.** There might not be a better time to talk about faith than at bedtime. Share the highs and lows from the day and then take time to pray for each other. With teenagers you can ask, "What's on your schedule tomorrow that I can pray for? Do any of your friends need prayer for anything?"

4. **Meal Time.** Taking a moment to give God thanks and praise before eating establishes a ritual that remains with children into adulthood. At the Bible camp where I grew up, we had a variety of mealtime prayers. Here are a few for you to choose from:

- *Johnny Appleseed.* "Oh, the Lord is good to me/ and so I thank the Lord/for giving me the things I need/the sun and the rain and the apple seed./The Lord is good to me./Amen."
- *God Is Great.* "God is great, God is good, and we thank Him for our food. We're gonna thank Him in the morning, noon and night. We're gonna thank our God 'cause He's out of sight. We're gonna thank our God 'cause He's dynamite. Amen."
- *God Beloved* (sung to the tune of "Are You Sleeping?"). "God beloved/God beloved/once again/once again/Thank You for our blessings/thank You for our blessings/A-A-men/A-A-men."
- *Doxology.* "Be present at our table, Lord/Be here and everywhere adored./These mercies bless and grant that we/may strengthened for Thy service be./Amen."
- *For Life and Health.* "For life and health and every good we give You thanks, O Lord."

- *Come, Lord Jesus.* "Come, Lord Jesus, be our guest
and let these gifts to us be blessed. Amen."

5. **Vacation Time.** Traveling together over a long distance or just getting away on a long weekend trip can
be a great time to reestablish faith-talk in your family. Tithe 10 percent of your vacation time to God. Do
a family service project, take some quiet time to read
the Bible together, or have a family devotion each
day. Visit another church and discuss what you liked
and disliked. On the final evening of your vacation,
spend time in prayer and worship. This doesn't have
to be elaborate—simply listen to a few contemporary
Christian songs and take some time to give thanks
for the time you've spent together. Take turns sharing one thing that you were thankful for on the trip
and one thing you look forward to when you get home.

6. **Memory-Making Time.** As a youth and family pastor, I had opportunities to lead many youth-service
trips. These trips were often life changing times for
the teens as they experienced being the hands and
feet of Jesus. While I loved leading these service trips,
I always wondered what could happen if families
shared these experiences together. If your family is
having relational conflicts, think about doing a service project together. The shared experience of helping those less fortunate than yourselves will probably
give all of you a new perspective on the problems that
your family is facing.

7. **One-on-One Time.** I think just about every parent
says the same thing about their kids: "They grow up
so fast." Soon, you'll be wondering where the time
went. We have a refrigerator magnet that reads "Don't

should on yourself," which means don't go through life saying, "I should have done that." One of the best things that you can do as a parent is to establish the ritual of one-on-one time with each of your children. It can be weekly or monthly, but it needs to be built in to your life rhythm. A failure to establish this time will leave you saying later in life, "I should have done that." Spend a weekend alone with each of your children, or establish a monthly date night when you see a movie or have dinner together. The particular activity is far less important than your commitment to spend time together.[10]

The reality is that you do have time to talk about faith with your children. You just need to take advantage of some of these slices of time. Yes, you're busy, but keep in mind that time is what you make of it.

R—Repetition

One of the keys to faith-talk is repetition. Do you know what the word "deuteronomy" means? (It's okay, neither did I!) It means "repetition of the law." If you read all of Deuteronomy, you'll find that Moses continually repeats the basic commands of God to a very stubborn group of people who wanted to live life their own way instead of God's. Does that sound familiar? Perhaps we need a similar teaching style today in which we continually repeat the basic truths of God to our children.

Rolf Garborg, author of *The Family Blessing*, started a ritual of saying a blessing over his daughter every evening.[11] When his daughter was an infant, he would go into her room as she was sleeping and say a blessing over her. As his daughter grew older, he continued the blessing ritual throughout her teenage years. Rolf admits that during one period of time when his daughter was a teenager, he would again wait until she was asleep to give her the blessing. But he kept up the ritual.

Rolf and his wife dreaded the day that they would have to leave their daughter at college. To make it through that day, they came up with a plan to unload her stuff, quickly say their good-byes in the dorm room and then grab each other's hands to head for the car with no looking back.

The plan worked to perfection—until they were almost to their car. In the distance behind them, they heard, "Mom, Dad, wait." Rolf and his wife stopped in their tracks and turned around, and as their daughter came running up to them with tears in her eyes, she said, "You forgot to bless me." Right there in the parking lot, Rolf and his wife huddled together with their daughter and said, "May the Lord continue to bless you and keep you. May the Lord continue to make His face shine on you and be gracious to you. May the Lord continue to look upon you with favor and give you peace. In the name of the Father, Son and Holy Spirit. Amen."

> Effective faith-talk is as much about listening and receiving as it is about talking and giving.

Guess what my wife and I started doing immediately after we heard this story? Before Malyn goes to bed, Maria repeats the above blessing to her. Malyn hears this blessing every evening. If we're separated for an evening, Maria will share the blessing over the phone. There have even been occasions when Malyn has said, "Don't forget to bless me, Mom!"

A—Acceptance

Effective faith-talk is as much about listening and receiving as it is about talking and giving. All of us are growing in our relationship with Christ, and no one has all the answers. Accept your children and the unique gifts that God has given to them. God has a purpose and plan for them—and His plan may not be the same as your plan for their lives.

In the same way, children need to learn to accept their parents as the people God has given them to shape and mold their lives. You're not perfect, but you should stress to your children that God commands that they accept and love you. "Children, obey your parents in the Lord, for this is right. 'Honor your father and mother'—which is the first commandment with a promise—'that it may go well with you and that you may enjoy long life on the earth'" (Eph. 6:1-3).

My mom and dad have been lifelong examples of this to me. From the day I was born, my parents accepted the call that God had on my life. When I felt God leading me to take a year off after high school before going to college, my parents accepted my decision. They rejoiced when I graduated from college. And they accepted each call I received in ministry—even the call to pastor a church in California, which meant taking their one and only granddaughter 2,000 miles away!

However, it was on one of the darkest days in my life that I felt their acceptance the most. I'd just finished the last final of my sophomore year in college. My car was packed and I was ready to make the 90-minute drive home. My roommate asked me to join him at the campus bar for appetizers and a beer before I left. Before I knew it a few hours went by—and a few beers as well. As I prepared to leave, my roommate admonished me to stay because he thought I'd had too many drinks to drive. But I ignored him and went on my way.

As I headed out of town, a police car pulled up behind me. I wasn't swerving or speeding, so I thought that the officer would eventually turn away. But after a mile or so, the officer turned on his lights and pulled me over. When he came to the window, he asked me to get out of the car. I asked him what I'd done, but he didn't reply.

Eventually, I was asked to take a breathalyzer test. When the police officer read the results, he told me to put my hands behind my back, because I was being arrested for DUI (Driving Under the Influence). Later that evening, as I sat in a cell room, I was overcome with the feeling that I'd let my parents down. I would have to tell them what happened.

I was allowed to make one phone call, but I couldn't bring myself to call my parents. So I called my sister in Chicago, and all we did was cry together. I was completely humiliated and devastated, and I didn't sleep at all that night. The next morning, I was released.

The 90-minute drive home turned into a three-hour drive. I couldn't bear the thought of facing my parents. When I pulled into the driveway, I couldn't even get out of the car. I was ready to hand them the keys and take whatever punishment they wanted to give me.

Then something happened that I never expected. My mom and dad came running out of the house to the car, opened the door, wrapped their arms around me and said, "Mark, we love you so much! We're glad you're okay. Come in—we have a big meal waiting for you. We love you, and we'll help you get through this."

I think at that moment, for the first time, I really understood the unconditional love of God. I realized that my parents not only accepted me in the good times, but they also accepted me in my lowest times.

I—Intentionality

Faith-talk requires that we intentionally involve ourselves in the lives of our children. Many parents have said to me, "My teenager won't talk to me. She won't tell me what's going on in her life." My reply is usually pretty blunt: "Try again! And don't stop until she talks to you."

When my wife, Maria, was a freshman in college, she informed her parents that she intended to quit school at the end of the year. This didn't sit well with them, because they'd worked hard to save enough money for her to attend a four-year private college. Over spring break, Maria's dad asked if she would help him with some roofing work that he was doing on the garage. It wasn't unusual for her to help her dad with projects like this, so Maria climbed up the ladder to the garage roof. "Where do we start, Dad?" she asked.

Maria's dad walked over to the ladder and kicked it off the garage—meaning they had no way down. He sat next to Maria and said, "It's time for us to have a talk about you and college."

To make a long story short, after the talk, Maria committed to completing college. But what she remembers more than the ladder crashing to the ground was that her dad cared enough to talk with her about her struggles in college. She'll always be grateful that he intentionally involved himself in her life struggles.

Effective faith-talk will probably require you to have some uncomfortable discussions with your kids. Often the discomfort occurs when you're forced to confront your own sinful behaviors and attitudes. After my DUI, my dad intentionally involved himself in my life by having an honest discussion with me about the dangers of alcoholism. He'd only been free from his own alcoholism for a few years, but he spoke God's truth in love to me. As a result, I was able to avoid heading down the same road. Effective faith-talk occurs when you intentionally involve Christ in all the areas of your life—and in the good times and the bad.

N—Never Ending

My dad once said to me, "You never stop being a parent." In the same way, faith-talk is a never-ending dialogue with your children.

I've found that the power of sharing God's story grows even stronger through the years. A few years ago, during my family's summer vacation, I had the opportunity to hear my dad preach. He was filling in for a pastor who was on vacation. At the time, I didn't know that this would be the last time I would hear him preach before he passed away. But while I always enjoyed hearing my dad preach, it was my mother who taught me something on this particular Sunday. After Dad's sermon, the organist started playing the hymn "I Love to Tell the Story." As we were standing to sing, my mom leaned over to me with a smile on her face and said, "This was your grandpa's favorite hymn."

I never knew my grandpa—her dad—because he died when I was very young. Yet I know him through my mom. I know that he was a man who had a very strong faith, because he shared this faith with her. At some point, he'd told my mom that "I Love to Tell the Story" was his favorite hymn, and she passed this on to me. And now, when this hymn is played in my church, I love to lean over to my daughter and tell her, "This was your great grandpa's favorite hymn." Although my grandfather has passed away, his faith continues on through his children and his children's children.

Take every chance you can to practice faith-talk with your children—and remember that faith-talk doesn't need to end when they grow up and are on their own. You can make a lasting impression on your children and the generations of children that follow.

Notes

1. George Barna, *Transforming Children Into Spiritual Champions* (Ventura, CA: Regal Books, 2003), p. 42.
2. Search Institute is a nonprofit, nonsectarian research and educational organization that advances the well-being and positive development of children and youth through applied research, evaluation, consultation, training, and the development of publications and practical resources for educators, youth-serving professionals, parents, community leaders and policy makers. Phone: 1-800-888-7828. Website: www.search-institute.org.

3. Search Institute, "Introduction to Assets," *Search Institute Home*, 2005. http://www.search-institute.org/assets/ (accessed September 2, 2005).

4. Copyright © 1997 by Search Institute SM. All rights reserved. Reprinted with permission. No other use of this chart is permitted without prior permission from Search Institute, 615 First Avenue NE, Minneapolis, MN 55413; www.search-institute.org.

5. Reprinted with permission. Copyright © 1997 by Search Institute SM. All rights reserved. No other use is permitted without prior permission from Search Institute, 615 First Avenue NE, Minneapolis, MN 55413; www.search-institute.org.

6. Reprinted with permission. Copyright © 1997 by Search Institute SM. All rights reserved. No other use is permitted without prior permission from Search Institute, 615 First Avenue NE, Minneapolis, MN 55413; www.search-institute.org.

7. Reprinted with permission from *Effective Christian Education: A National Study of Protestant Congregations.* Copyright © 1990 by Search Institute SM. No other use is permitted without prior permission from Search Institute, 615 First Avenue NE, Minneapolis, MN 55413; www.search-institute.org.

8. Barna, *Transforming Children*, p. 78.

9. Dr. Roland Martinson serves as the professor of pastoral care and theology at Luther Seminary in St. Paul, Minnesota. The Youth and Family Institute is a nonprofit organization that presents a partnership of family and congregation in which the home is viewed as the primary place for teaching and nurturing the faith through conferences, consultation, training, and development of publications and practical resources for pastors, youth educators and church professionals. Website: www.youthandfamilyinstitute.org.

10. Dr. Roland Martinson shared these seven opportunities at a Child in Our Hands conference sponsored by the Youth and Family Institute.

11. For information on *The Family Blessing*, contact Rolf Garborg, 4090-145th Street, Prior Lake, MN 55372. Phone: 612-440-7780.

Child Makeover Keys

Key 1: It's all about faith! The most important thing children need in their lives is faith—a personal relationship with Jesus. You're called to pass on the faith to your children and to your children's children.

Key 2: If you want your children to have a faith that sticks, they need to see it modeled in the home. One-hour-a-week Christianity will not lead to a faith that is firmly impressed on the hearts of your children.

Key 3: Faith talk can happen anytime and anywhere. Bring faith talk into your home, into your car, on your vacation and so forth.

Key 4: Passing on the faith to your children requires you to T.R.A.I.N. them—with Time, Repetition, Acceptance, Intentionality and a Never-Ending attitude.

Family Activities

ACTIVITY 1
Faith-Talk

A great game is available through the Youth and Family Institute (www.youthandfamilyinstitute.org) called FaithTalk™. The game fits nicely into the glove compartment of your car. You can use it to stimulate faith-oriented discussions with your children.

The game has four sets of cards, one for each category: memories, actions, values and etchings. Some sample questions are:

- What is the one trait of your mother or father you value the most?
- Did you resent having to go to Sunday School as a child?
- What is one thing you would like to do before you die?
- Talk about something that happened to you recently that made you pause and thank God.

These questions will make for some great family discussions. There are two versions of the game: FaithTalk™ (for older children) and FaithTalk™ With Children (for younger children between the ages of 3 to 11). I encourage you to get a copy of FaithTalk™ and use it to stimulate your family's faith.

ACTIVITY 2
Praying Together

Perhaps you've never prayed with your children. But no matter how old they are, it's never too late to start. It helps to remember that prayer is simply a conversation with God.

Here are a few ideas to get you started.

1. *Newspaper Prayer.* Try this idea at the beginning of the day as you're eating breakfast. Have each family member take a portion of the newspaper and circle items that he or she feels need to be prayed for. Then ask family members to pray for the things they circled in the paper.

2. *Sentence Prayer.* You can help your children pray aloud by giving them a sentence to complete, such as:

   - "Lord, I thank you for . . . "
   - "Lord, forgive me for . . . "
   - "Lord, help my friend . . . "
   - "Lord, help me be more . . . "
   - "Lord, help me to let go of . . . "
   - "Lord, give me the courage to . . . "
   - "Lord, one of the fears I need help with is . . . "

3. *Highs and Lows.* Ask your children what their "highs" were from the day, and then ask them about their "lows" from the day. Share your highs and lows as well, and then pray for them together.

4. *Prayer Journal.* Share your prayer requests with the other members of your family and then record them in a prayer journal. One person can pray for all the

requests you've listed for the day. The next time you pray together, look over the requests you listed previously and update any changes and answers. This is a good way to see how God has been active in your prayer lives.

5. *A.C.T.S. Prayer.* This is a well-known form of prayer that is easy to remember.

- *A* stands for "adoration." Begin the prayer by simply adoring God for who He is.
- *C* stands for "confession." Spend some time confessing your sins.
- *T* stands for "thanksgiving." Take time to thank God for the blessings that He has given to you and your family.
- *S* stands for "supplication." Lift up specific areas of your life in which you need God to supply for your needs.

ACTIVITY 3
Family Service Project

If you want to make a lasting memory for your family, do a service project together. This could be as simple as going to an elderly person's home and doing yard work or participating in a roadside cleanup project.

The project isn't as important as the act of doing service together. Find something your family is comfortable with and get busy. You won't be disappointed. In fact, you'll quickly discover that you will receive more than you give.

To help you get started, consider the following:

- What could your family do, without being asked, to help a neighbor?
- What could your family do to help preserve God's creation and care for it?
- What is something that your family could do to help at church?
- What could you give away, and to whom could you give it?

Small-Group Discussion Starters

1. Think about the people who influenced you during your developmental years. What role did they play (or not play) in the development of your faith?

2. How much faith-talk did you experience growing up? What form did it take? When did it happen? Who started it?

3. Go through the 40 Developmental Assets chart in this chapter and discuss how your children are doing in these areas. How many assets do you think they have?

4. If "religious community" (which fosters personal faith) is the most important asset, how is faith being taught or caught in your home?

CHAPTER 4

The Extended Family Makeover

When I was about 25 years old, I moved into church ministry as a youth and family ministry pastor. On many occasions, I felt like I was in over my head. One such occasion was when a teenaged girl from our church died suddenly of heart failure on New Year's Eve.

Lana was a spirited girl who had been born with a bad heart. She lived with a pacemaker for her entire life—although I had absolutely no idea this was the case until she attended a youth retreat I was leading. As kids arrived and got loaded onto the bus, Lana's mom pulled me aside and said, "I need to talk to you for a minute before you leave." She then discreetly informed me about Lana's heart condition and what they'd been dealing with since she had been born. As for the retreat, she said, "If you do any rigorous activity, she may need to slow down and catch her breath a little. I just want you to be aware so that you can keep an eye on her."

Lana and I had a fun relationship. I needled her and she was good with the comebacks. Lana was a bit of a tomboy who loved to get herself in the middle of everything that the boys in the group were doing.

At the retreat, as we were getting ready to play some touch football, I saw my opportunity to get in a shot at Lana. She was putting on her jacket to head out to join the boys in playing football, so I said, "Lana, where are you going?"

She simply replied, "To play football!"

I seized the opportunity and responded, "You can't play football. You're a girl!" If looks could kill, I would have been dead at that moment and not writing this book!

Lana looked at me with her hands on her hips and dramatically exclaimed, "Well, I never!" But before she could finish, I went over and put her in a headlock. And in a fit of laughter, off we went to play.

Later that same year—in fact, in the middle of the night on New Year's Eve—the phone rang at my home. It was Lana's mom. Barely able to speak, she informed me that Lana's pacemaker had failed during the night and that Lana had passed away. I was devastated.

On the day of the funeral service, I still had no idea what I was going to say to the family and friends who would be filling our church. I picked up the phone and called my dad. For the next 45 minutes, he shared with me similar situations he'd faced in ministry. While he didn't tell me what to say, he guided me to a place in Scripture where I found the words I needed to share.

That evening, as I was driving home, I called him back and tearfully told him how thankful I was to have him as my dad. I thanked him for giving me the passion to want to be a pastor and for being my role model, mentor and best friend.

I don't know how Maria and I would have made it this far—in our marriage and as parents—if it hadn't been for the wisdom, counsel, support and guidance of our parents and other elders who've come alongside us as a family. Yet I see so many families today who seem to have nowhere to turn for advice when times get tough.

One of the greatest resources we have as parents is the wisdom of our parents, extended family and others who have gone through the ups and downs of family life before us. Many members of older generations grew up at a time when the home was still a place where faith was nurtured through conversations, Bible reading, devotions, prayer or family service projects. They may be the last generation who experienced that faith nurture in the home. Who better to teach us today than the generation who lived through it? Unfortunately, most of us today don't make use of this resource and opportunity.

Missing Out

For many parents, distance has reduced or eliminated the role that grandparents have traditionally played in the lives of children. Often, the grandchild-grandparent relationship is limited to Christmas and birthday cards, occasional phone conversations and an annual visit. I didn't have much of a relationship with my grandparents because they lived in northern Minnesota and we lived in Illinois. Fortunately, I had a great-aunt and a great-uncle who lived in Chicago and who filled the role of grandparents in my life.

Thankfully, things seem to be getting better again. Through e-mail, cell phones and even web cams, grandparents and their families are able to stay more closely connected even though many miles separate them. While distance was a major issue in the past, it no longer needs to be today, because technology can close the gap for families.

Unfortunately, however, many of us don't seek the wisdom and counsel of older generations because we don't think that our parents will be able to relate to how different life is today. We usually think things like, *I can't talk to them because they just don't understand. Things were different then.* I realize that the world is changing at a very rapid pace. If you wanted advice on how to load your iPod or add a memory chip to your computer, I would generally steer you away from the elder generation. But when it comes to passing on faith to our children, we can learn a lot from our elders. This is the generation that has watched the slow disintegration of the family over the past several decades, and they've lived through what works and what doesn't work when it comes to nurturing the Christian faith. Isn't this the very wisdom that we're looking for?

I remember when Gus came into my office and said, "Pastor, I need to talk with you." When he closed the door, I began to get nervous! But then he sat down and said, "Each month, I'm going to write you a check, and I want you to use the money to help families. I don't want anyone to know where the money is coming from, and I don't want to know whom you choose to help. I just want you to use it to help families in need."

I was moved by Gus's passion and commitment. Of course, I thanked him for his generosity. But then I looked at him and said, "I need to ask you one question. Why are you doing this?"

Gus sat back in his chair and was silent for a few minutes. Then, with a pained expression on his face, he opened up his heart to me. "I didn't do the greatest job raising my kids, but I did the best job I knew how at the time. They're grown and now have kids of their own, and it saddens me to say that they're not involved with God or the church. One of my kids has been through a divorce, and the other one is caught up in the fast pace of life. We really don't talk that much because they're always too busy and clearly don't want our help. So I figure that if I can't help them, maybe I can help some other families."

Gus was willing to admit the mistakes he had made as a parent, and he even wanted to encourage his adult children not to do things the way that he had done them. Unfortunately, his children weren't giving him the opportunity. But before we shake our heads at Gus's kids, we need to examine our own hearts. I think that many of us have a tendency to dismiss members of older generations too quickly, robbing ourselves and our families of an invaluable source of wisdom, counsel and support.

> Many of us have a tendency to dismiss members of older generations too quickly, robbing ourselves and our families of an invaluable source of wisdom, counsel and support.

Of course, I don't think that the entire blame can be placed on parents today, as some of the blame rests with the elder generation for not taking more initiative to be involved in the lives of their children and their children's children. Many have too willingly stepped aside with an attitude of "No one really cares what I have to say anyway, so I'll just sit back and let them make their own mistakes."

A woman I talked with once named Eleanor is a great example of a grandma who took the initiative to get involved. It was late summer and many parents were registering their teenagers for "confirmation," a junior high youth ministry program in our church. One afternoon, I received an interesting phone call. "Pastor Mark, my name is Eleanor," the voice on the other end of the line said. "I'm not a member of your congregation, but my daughter and son-in-law attend your church."

I thanked Eleanor for calling and asked what I could do for her. "Well, I'm a little embarrassed," she said. "You see, my daughter and son-in-law aren't at church frequently, but because of my insistence they've made sure that my precious grandson attends Sunday School there every week." She continued, hesitating a bit. "The reason I'm calling is that my grandson is entering sixth grade. As I understand, this is the year that you begin your junior high confirmation program. While I probably have no right to ask you to look into this for me, I was wondering whether you could tell me if my grandson is registered for confirmation."

At that point, I remember thinking to myself, *No right! She has every right to ask this question!* In fact, I complimented her for caring enough to call. "Eleanor, I think it's great that you care so much about the faith life of your children and grandchildren. You understand the importance of passing on the faith to your children and their children. I wish I had hundreds of grandparents who would call me with the same question that you've asked."

I waited for her reply, thinking that she would appreciate the compliment, but she simply responded, "Are you going to look it up?" Talk about a focused grandparent! I did find that her grandson was indeed registered for the class. I then added, "You can call me anytime, Eleanor, and we'll pray together that your family will grow in their faith in the Lord."

While Eleanor's call makes for a great story, in all my years of ministry, it's the *only* phone call like this that I have received from a grandparent. It seems that I should receive hundreds of phone calls like this! We need meddling elders in the lives of our families, and I strongly encourage grandparents everywhere to meddle in the faith life of their children and children's children!

Psalm 78:2-8 provides all the inspiration that members of older generations should need:

I will open my mouth in parables, I will utter hidden things, things from of old—what we have heard and known, what our fathers have told us. We will not hide them from their children; we will tell the next generation the praiseworthy deeds of the LORD, his power, and the wonders he has done. He decreed statutes for Jacob and established the law in Israel, which he commanded our forefathers to teach their children, so the next generation would know them, even the children yet to be born, and they in turn would tell their children. Then they would put their trust in God and would not forget his deeds but would keep his commands. They would not be like their forefathers—a stubborn and rebellious generation, whose hearts were not loyal to God, whose spirits were not faithful to him.

What this psalm is telling us is that when the elder generation disengages from active involvement and participation in nurturing the faith of today's families, they lose, we lose, our children lose, and our children's children lose. Did you get that? No one wins! And the result of this disengagement is a "stubborn and rebellious generation, whose hearts are not loyal to God." Does that sound familiar? Parents need to seek out the wisdom and direction of their elders. And elders must not "hide," but instead take a prominent and active role in the lives of their families.

It's Time for a Change

One of the greatest fears I have as Malyn grows up is about the choices that she will make regarding dating and, eventually, marriage. I've ordered her to stop growing, but she just doesn't listen!

Recently, I performed the wedding of a great young couple—both of whom were Christians and completely in love with God and each other. It was one of those types of relationships that you desire for your own child. I said to the father of the bride,

"You must be relieved that your daughter found such a good man to be her husband."

His response surprised me. "I take no credit for that," he said. "My parents and my wife's parents have been praying for my daughter's eventual husband since the day she was born. I believe that this marriage—and the fact that my daughter made good dating decisions—is a direct answer to their prayers."

Bells immediately began ringing in my mind! What if we released our elder generation to be continually in prayer for our children and our families? Could we see a major transformation in families today? I believe the answer is a resounding yes, because the Bible says that God loves to answer our prayers. "Then you will call, and the LORD will answer; you will cry for help, and he will say: Here am I" (Isa. 58:9). "In that day you will no longer ask me anything. I tell you the truth, my Father will give you whatever you ask in my name. Until now you have not asked for anything in my name. Ask and you will receive, and your joy will be complete" (John 16:23-24).

Have you asked God to protect your children and family? Have you asked your parents and grandparents to pray for you and your children? Do you give your parents, on some sort of regular basis, your family's prayer requests and needs? You probably have many other older folks in your church who would gladly fill this role for you if you simply asked them to do so.

It seems like we love to complain about our children or our family situation, yet we won't proactively do anything about it. Just about every family-oriented sitcom shows parents fighting with one another. The children complain about their parents and parents complain about their children. In this case, "art" seems to imitate life. A lot of us are great at complaining about our situation, but we're not tapping into the one source that can change it.

We have the God of the universe in our lives, who has the ability to create all that exists by speaking a word. He has the power to part the Red Sea and He can move mountains. Yet we don't turn to

Him to help us with our family problems. Instead—as I mentioned earlier in the book—we go searching the Internet, or we turn on Oprah or Dr. Phil and expect them to transform our families. Let's see, if you ask me to choose between Dr. Phil and God, whom should I choose? Dr. Phil may offer good advice, but I'll take God every time!

In the next decade, we are going to begin to see the largest demographic group in American history, Baby Boomers, begin to retire. Over the past three decades, we've seen the steady erosion of the family. But what would happen if parents today would simply ask, empower and release the Baby Boomer generation to pray for their children and their children's families? I think we would see a transformation of epic proportions!

> If parents today would simply ask, empower and release the Baby Boomer generation to pray for their children and their children's families, we would see a transformation of epic proportions!

The Promise of Grandpa Moses

Look at Deuteronomy 6:1-2 one more time. It's intriguing to realize that Moses was speaking from a grandfather's perspective to people of a younger generation who were parenting children. Listen to his grandfatherly wisdom:

> These are the commands, decrees and laws [There is one true God. Love God with all of your heart, soul and strength (see vv. 4-5)] the LORD your God directed me to teach you to observe . . . so that you, your children and their children after them may fear the LORD your God as long as you live by keeping all his decrees and commands that I give you, and so that you may enjoy long life.

Do you hear Moses' advice? He is clearly telling us God's will for enjoying long life! Isn't this exactly what we want most for our children, our children's children and ourselves? It's certainly what I want most for my daughter. I want Malyn to enjoy her life and to be happy, content, supported, at peace and loved. Moses is saying that God wants all these things for her as well. If Malyn understands and follows the basic will and commands of God, she'll enjoy her life no matter what comes her way. What a comforting promise for us as parents!

Don't get me wrong. I'm not saying that life is guaranteed to be easy. Scripture is also clear that difficulties will come our way, but these don't have to prevent us from enjoying life. "Consider it pure joy, my brothers [and sisters], whenever you face trials of many kinds" (Jas. 1:2).

Once again, my parents were a great example of this for me throughout my life. One situation in particular demonstrated to me how they always lived in joy and loved life in spite of trying times. In 1980, my parents were stopped at a traffic light when a construction truck lost its brakes and rammed into the back of their van. The force of the impact threw both of them to the back of the van. The injuries they sustained were life-altering.

Prior to this accident, my parents had been very active people. My dad was a Bible camp director who was always running around the camp, playing with kids or doing maintenance work. My mother served as camp cook, secretary and lawn mower. Still, she found time to play with me in a game of horse now and then.

Following the accident, my parents started down a road of health problems. My father had three back surgeries and a total of seven vertebrae fused together. My mother had neck, back and heart problems. Both were forced to retire early from a ministry they dearly loved. There was not a day that went by in which they were not dealing with pain or other related health problems. Yet they truly enjoyed life. They certainly didn't enjoy their health problems, but because of their faith and their understanding of God's will and commands, they didn't allow their declining health to prevent them from enjoying life.

In October 2004, I had my last visit with my dad before he passed away from heart and lung disease on November 23. As I was by his bedside in the intensive care unit, my dad received many visitors. As people would leave, he'd always say the same thing: "Don't grieve for me. Life is good because God is good!" Even from his hospital bed and in the final hours of his life, my dad continued to mentor me.

As I'm writing these words, it has only been six months since he left his earthly life and entered God's presence. And I am still grieving the loss of my dad, my mentor, my friend, my role model and my confidant. As the tears flow down my cheeks, I'm so grateful for the wisdom I received from him. I didn't just learn from what he did right, but I also learned from his mistakes. And when I got busy with life and didn't have time for him, he easily could have felt pushed aside or discounted. But he kept right on meddling in my life. He continued to ask how things were going, and he relentlessly prayed for my family. Like many people his age, he often repeated the same stories from his life experiences. Sometimes, I'd think to myself, *Here we go again!* Now that he's gone, I'd give anything to hear one of those stories again.

Reconnect and Reengage

God gave us our godly elders and extended families for a reason. Psalm 68:6 says, "God sets the lonely in families." God never intended for you to go through life alone. If you truly want to make over your family, it's time you and your family reconnected and reengaged with godly elders.

This may mean reaching out and giving permission to your godly parents and grandparents to meddle in your life again. Listen to them and learn from them because they have something valuable to share with you. Or you might need to ask someone to serve as a surrogate elder for you and your family. The word "family" has the same root as that of the word "familiar," so ask yourself, "Who is a familiar godly elder who could serve in this role for us?" In most churches there are many godly people who would love to serve you and your family in this way.

Recently, I was talking with a man who was about to turn 60. When I asked, "What does the future look like for you?" he responded, "I still want to be contributing when I'm 80." He and his wife do not have children of their own, but they've become "adopted" grandparents to a neighboring family's child. They even help pay for this boy to attend a private Christian school. Instead of sitting back and saying, "Look how bad things are for families today," this man and his wife are doing something about it by getting actively involved in the life of another family. They're passing on their faith and biblical wisdom, and a young family is benefiting from their commitment.

The Bible continually points out the importance of seeking out the wisdom and prayers of elders. James 5:14-15 states:

> Is any one of you sick? He should call the elders of the church to pray over him and anoint him with oil in the name of the Lord. And the prayer offered in faith will make the sick person well; the Lord will raise him up. If he has sinned, he will be forgiven.

Is your family hurting? Is it "sick" in some way? As I stated earlier, I believe that every family is dysfunctional. We're all sick and in need of healing. If you truly want healing—a family makeover—heed the Lord's reminder to incorporate godly elders in your family's life so that they can pray for you and you can receive healing.

Extended Family Makeover Keys

Key 1: God instituted the family as a multigenerational unit for a reason. All families need the wisdom and counsel of godly elders.

Key 2: Families need to be open to the counsel of godly elders. Encourage and actively pursue this kind of relationship. Don't be afraid to seek out their wisdom and guidance, especially when it comes to the difficult situations you're facing. Elders might just have the answer you need!

Key 3: Give godly elders permission to meddle in the lives of your family.

Key 4: Godly elders can be family members or "familiar" people who serve as extended family members. If you don't have a family member who can serve in this way, you can invite someone else to be an elder, advisor and friend to your family.

Family Activities

ACTIVITY 1
Baptism/Dedication Sponsors

Not that long ago, it was common practice for parents to name godparents for their children. The godparent served as a spiritual role model for the child.

Identify one or two people from the elder generation who could serve as godparents for your children. Invite them to assist you in the faith nurture of your child. Give them permission to meddle in your family's faith development. Ask them to contact you monthly and ask:

- How many times have you prayed together as a family this week?
- How many times have you worshiped together as a family this week?
- Have you recently done a service project together as a family?
- How much time have you spent in God's Word this month? What have you learned about God as a result?

ACTIVITY 2
Prayer Partner

Find a godly elder who can be a prayer partner for your family. This can be one person for the entire family or one prayer partner for each member of the family. Just as you'd maintain contact with a pen pal, submit your prayer requests to your prayer partner on a weekly basis. This can become a family activity in which you take a few moments to share prayer requests and then one member of the family sends the requests to your prayer partner via e-mail.

Provide a prayer journal for your prayer partner so that he or she can keep track of your requests. Over time you will see how God actively responds to your prayers.

ACTIVITY 3
Faith Mentors

A 1990 Search Institute report titled "Effective Christian Education: A National Study of Protestant Congregations" surveyed more than 11,000 participants in 561 congregations throughout the United States. The survey found a direct correlation between the maturity level of faith in teenagers and children and their opportunities to discuss faith issues with their parents and other adults. Unfortunately, the survey revealed that the percentage of youth who have a regular dialogue with an adult other than their parent on faith/life issues is only 4 percent.[1]

As your children grow into teenagers, they'll naturally begin to seek out the perspective and "voices" of other people. As a parent, the key questions for you are: Who will those other people be? Will they reinforce or contradict the values and behaviors you're seeking to instill and develop in your children? Rather than leaving the answers to these questions to chance, consider the significant role an adult faith mentor can play in the growth of your children during their difficult teenaged years.

In our congregation, we wanted to help parents of teenagers find faith mentors for their children. We started a six-week mentoring program for the purpose of building bridges between our teenagers and our elder generation. We gave the teens a month to find a faith mentor. We said that the mentor needed to be a certain age (if your church has enough older adults, set the age at 40, 50 or even 60), a member of our church, and not related to the teenager. For those teenagers who were unable to identify a mentor, we found a willing adult to mentor them. (Of course, we always paired a male mentor with a male teenager and female mentor with a female teenager.)

The teenagers and adult faith mentors were then asked to attend our worship service together for six weeks. After each service, they were to go through a simple discussion guide. At the end of the six weeks, we had the mentors and teenagers write and exchange thank-you letters to one another. It was obvious that many of these relationships had grown deep in just six weeks.

Look for a faith mentor for your teenager. If you need help finding a mentor, ask your pastor to help. Below are some mentoring guidelines and discussion guides to help you establish a faith-mentoring relationship between your teenager and another adult.

Selecting a Mentor

- 40+ years of age
- An extended family member or member of the church
- A person willing to listen, understand and accept your child
- A person committed to meeting for six consecutive weeks with your child

Faith-Mentoring Guidelines

- Mentors should establish the time, date and place of each meeting ahead of time with the parents. A good time might be immediately before or after church on Sundays.
- Meetings should be 30 to 45 minutes in length, but may vary if mutually agreed upon.
- Transportation of the child to and from meetings is the parent's responsibility. The parents must approve any transportation of the child by the mentor.
- The mentor should never meet one-on-one with a teen in a private place, but always in a public setting (such as a church foyer, sanctuary or restaurant).
- The meeting can take place in a teen's home if the parents

will also be home.

- The mentor should keep all matters of discussion confidential, unless otherwise agreed. Confidentiality is essential for building trust.
- If you are a mentor, remember that it's okay not to have all the answers. Allow plenty of opportunities for questions, make sure the conversation isn't one-sided, and don't be afraid of silence during your discussions.

Faith-Mentoring Discussion Guides

The following are six discussion guides that are designed to stimulate discussion and build a relationship between a teenager and an adult faith mentor.

Theme Verse, John 3:16: For God so loved the world that he gave his one and only Son, that whoever believes in him shall not perish but have eternal life.

Week 1: Getting to Know God

Opening Prayer: Dear God, we ask that You would bless us as our mentoring relationship begins. Please bless the time that we have together, and give us courage to speak openly and honestly with one another and to learn from one another. In Your name, Lord Jesus, we pray. Amen.

1. Read the theme verse, John 3:16.
2. What is the most difficult thing that you have done or tried to do?
3. If you had to tell someone who God is, would that be easy or difficult? Why?

4. List seven things that complete the statement "God is . . ."
5. Complete this sentence: "A reason I know God exists is . . ."
6. How close do you feel to God in your everyday life?

   a. "I feel closer to God when . . ."
   b. "Sometimes I feel God is far away when . . ."

7. If you could ask God one question, what would it be?

Closing Prayer. Share your highs and lows from the past week. Close by praying for each other.

Week 2: Getting to Know the World

Opening Prayer: Dear Lord, we thank You for the world in which we live. Please forgive us for the way we mistreat our world, and help us to bring about Your kingdom in all we do. In Jesus' name, we pray. Amen.

1. Read the theme verse, John 3:16.
2. If you could go anywhere in the world, where would you go?
3. If a reporter from another planet were to come to you and ask, "What is the greatest thing that has happened or is happening on your world?" what would your answer be?
4. How is the world different today from the way it was:

   a. 25 years ago?
   b. 100 years ago?
   c. 2,000 years ago, when Jesus was on the earth?

5. What are some of the changes that are good? What are some of the changes that aren't so good?

6. What do you imagine God thinks about our world today? What things would God like? What things would God not like?

7. What will be different in our world 25, 100 and 2,000 years from now?

8. What do you see happening with Christianity in the future? What's our role in keeping the Christian faith alive for the future?

Closing Prayer: Share your highs and lows from the past week. Close by praying for each other.

Week 3: One and Only

Opening Prayer: Dear God, we thank You for sending Your one and only Son to die for us. Help us to never forget what You did for us. In Your name, Lord Jesus, we pray. Amen.

1. Read the theme verse, John 3:16.

2. How many children are in your family? How many in your mother's and father's families?

3. If you have brothers or sisters, describe your relationship with them. If you don't have siblings, describe your relationship with your best friend.

4. What are some good things about being a son or daughter? What are some difficult things?

5. What do you think were some good things for Jesus as the Son of God? What would have been some potentially difficult things?

6. If something tragic were to happen to you or to one of your family members, how would you feel?

7. How do you think God felt when He watched His

one and only Son be crucified? Why did God let this happen?

Closing Prayer: Share your highs and lows from the past week. Close by praying for each other.

Week 4: Believe Me!

Opening Prayer: Dear Lord, You've given us many reasons to believe in You. Please help us to believe and obey You in all areas of our lives. In Your name, we pray. Amen.

1. Read the theme verse, John 3:16.
2. How would you define the word "believe"?
3. Complete this sentence: "Some things I believe in are . . ."
4. Now complete this sentence: "Some things I don't believe in are . . ."
5. How would you complete this statement? "Some things I used to believe in but no longer do are . . ."
6. Who are the people you believe when they tell you something? Why do you believe them?
7. If you wanted someone to believe you, how would you do it?
8. If someone were to ask you, "Do you believe in God?" how would you respond?
9. What has God done to make it easier for people to believe in Him?
10. In what ways is God still doing things today to help people believe in Him?

Closing Prayer: Share your highs and lows from the past week. Close by praying for each other.

Week 5: Death Changes Things

Opening Prayer: God, we know that in all things You work for good and that even in death we who believe in the death and resurrection of Jesus have life. Please help us to handle death as it surrounds us and to help those who have been affected by the death of loved ones. In Your name, Lord Jesus, we pray. Amen.

1. Recite the theme verse, John 3:16, from memory.
2. Have you (or someone you know) ever had an experience in which you thought you might die?
3. How did this experience change or affect you?
4. If you had one week to live, what would you do? Why?
5. What prevents you from doing those things today?
6. Have you ever lost a loved one or someone you were close to? How did this make you feel?
7. The theme verse says, "Whoever believes in him shall not perish." What does that mean? How does this change your outlook on life and death?

Closing Prayer: Share your highs and lows from the past week. Close by praying for each other.

Week 6: Life Everlasting!

Opening Prayer: Dear God, we thank You for the time we've had to get to know one another these past six weeks. Please continue to draw us closer to You and to each other in the days, weeks and years ahead. In Your name, Jesus, we pray. Amen.

1. Recite the theme verse, John 3:16, from memory.
2. What is the best Christmas or birthday gift that you've ever received?

3. If you could ask for any gift this year for Christmas, what would it be?

4. What do you think heaven is like? What does it look like? Who's there?

5. Do people your age think that the gift of heaven is better than any gift we could receive here on Earth? Why or why not?

6. If the person sitting across from you were to give you the gift you wanted in question 3, how would you respond? If the person sitting across from you were willing to give that same gift to someone else, to whom would you want that gift to be given?

7. Anyone who believes in Jesus Christ receives the free gift of eternal life. What do you think this means? How do you respond to this?

8. That gift is also available to anyone you know. Who are you telling about this free gift?

9. Who is someone you know who currently isn't a Christian but who you wish would become a Christian?

10. What can you do (or have you done) to help him or her know the love of Jesus Christ?

Closing Prayer: Share your highs and lows from the past week. Close by praying for each other.

Ongoing Mentoring Resource

If the six-week mentoring program goes well and you want to continue, a good resource is *The Youth Bible* from Word Publishing. *The Youth Bible* includes a variety of topics that you can read about together, including anger, depression, doubt, drugs and alcohol, friends, judging others and peer pressure.

Each topic has a variety of Scripture texts to examine as well as personal stories and illustrations written by teenagers.

Note

1. Survey results reprinted with permission from *Effective Christian Education: A National Study of Protestant Congregations.* Copyright © 1990 by Search Institute SM. No other use is permitted without prior permission from Search Institute, 615 First Avenue NE, Minneapolis, MN 55413; www.search-institute.org.

Small-Group Discussion Starters

1. Who are some of the people you look up to in life?
2. What role do elders (parents, grandparents and other members of older generations) play in the life of your family?
3. Who are your personal mentors, and who are your spiritual mentors?
4. What role do you want to play in the life of your children's children?

CHAPTER 5

The Church Makeover

Not long ago, my wife, Maria, was reading a magazine article as she ran on the treadmill. The article was about how to add 30 minutes to your day. The last suggestion almost made her fall off the treadmill. One woman proudly stated that she'd found a way to get two hours more out of her week by dropping her kids off at church and running errands while they were in Sunday School! The article pointed out a startling reality that for many families today, the church is no more than a safe "drop off" center for kids. I don't think this was God's intention when He created the Church.

I agree with researcher George Barna when he writes, "The local church should be an intimate and valuable partner in the effort to raise the coming generation of Christ's followers and church leaders, but it is the parents whom God will hold primarily accountable for the spiritual maturation of their children."[1] The key word for me in his statement is "partner." While I wholeheartedly believe that the local church can be the MVP—the "most valuable partner"—for families, I'm convinced that the church also needs a makeover.

What's Happened to the Church?

One reason why the local church is no longer seen as a valuable partner for families isn't really a problem with the church at all. It's the reality that families no longer seem to have time for church. Just a few decades ago, the church played a much more significant role in the lives of families. It wasn't unusual to see businesses closed on Sundays, and public schools wouldn't give homework on Wednesdays because that night was "church night." Families were committed to being at church whenever the doors were open.

Today, however, hardly anyone even recognizes the concept of "church night." Sunday morning is business as usual. If anything, the church now competes with sports leagues and many other extracurricular activities that vie for the family's time—even on Sunday mornings. I believe that Satan knows that the Christian Church is one of the most valuable resources families need in order to succeed. So he'll do everything he can to keep people from getting connected to an intentional Christian community. One of the tools he uses is to keep families so busy that they don't have time for church. And quite simply, when you don't have time for church, you can't establish a lasting partnership with the church.

Another problem is that many families don't recognize the local church as a resource to help them with their family relationships. People today will turn to TV and radio shrinks, the Internet, counseling and even medication to help them as a family. But the church isn't even a blip on their radar.

I once worked with a family who'd been through an ugly divorce. The parents battled almost every situation through lawsuits and court cases. They tried counseling but quit out of frustration. As is often the case, the children found themselves continually in the middle of their parents' warfare.

I became involved in the situation because the teenaged daughter in the family, Abby, started attending our youth worship service at the invitation of a school friend. Eventually, Abby joined a small group and began to open up. Things came to a head one Friday night when she came to church and asked to meet with me. She informed me that her mom was home, drunk, because she'd just had another fight with her ex-husband. Abby didn't know what to do. We called her mom and got permission for her to stay at her friend's house that evening.

The next day, I went over to meet with Abby's mom. When I arrived, I was greeted rather abruptly with "Who are you and what do you want?"

"My name is Pastor Mark," I said as politely as I could. "Abby is part of our youth group, and I was wondering if we could talk for a minute."

Somewhat surprised and a bit ashamed, Abby's mother responded more softly, "I'm sorry, I thought you were a door-to-door salesman." She invited me in, and after a few minutes I informed her that Abby had told me about the ugly divorce and the drinking problem she had. I asked if there was anything I could do to help.

The look of brokenness in her eyes said it all, and she struggled to reply. I looked her in the eyes and said softly, "Ma'am, I'm not here to judge you or to preach to you. I just want you to know that you, your children and even your ex-husband matter to God. And we'd welcome the opportunity to show you how Christ wants to help you and your family."

Abby's mom then broke into tears, and after a few moments she replied, "I used to go to church before all this happened. But after all of this mess, I thought the church was only for families who had it all together and that I no longer was welcome or belonged."

Over the course of the next two years, our church was able to come alongside this family and see God work many miracles. Abby now attends a Christian college and is studying to become a youth pastor. Her mom has made a complete turnaround and is now remarried to a wonderful Christian man.

While Abby's story is great news, the point I'm trying to make is that the Church needs to get back on the radar for families. If it hadn't been for Abby, her mom probably would never have set foot in her local church during her time of crisis and need. Whether she was right or wrong, she had the Church pegged as a place only for families that are healthy and "have it together." The Church as a whole needs to break this stereotype and put out a welcome mat that reads "*All* families are welcome here"!

Jesus as the Center

I once read a *USA Today* article that described the different forms of family that exist in our culture today. For example, a single mother is one form of family. A dual income, no kids (DINK) couple is another form of family. Do you know how many forms of family this article identified? Twenty-eight! While we could argue the strengths and weaknesses of each form of family, I can tell you with certainty that each form of family needs the same thing to succeed: Jesus Christ in the center of their family life!

Where are you going to learn about that and see it in action? From the media? In public schools? Unfortunately not, which is why you need the local church. George Barna writes, "It is true, though, that a family can benefit from the help of a supportive community [the church], especially when that community is grounded in the Christian faith—a faith that is genuine, unchanging, readily accessible, focused on what matters to God and based on love and truth."[2]

When I lead a new-member class at our church, I strongly stress the importance of the church as a partner to families. I begin by saying, "If you're looking for a place where you can drop off your children and expect us to teach them the faith, then you need to look for another church, because we're not the right church for you." I continue by explaining that our church believes the home is the primary place where faith is nurtured and that parents are to be the primary nurturers.

> The role of the church is to be a valuable and necessary partner to families.

While we believe this unwavering-ly, our church also recognizes that the majority of families today probably have no idea how to make their home a place for nurturing the faith of their children. So we desire to come alongside them, as a lifelong partner, and equip them to bring the love of Jesus Christ into the center of their homes and family life. We believe that only this will lead to families being healthy and whole.

"If you need to know how to pray in the home, we'll teach you," I explain to the new-member class. "If you need to know how to do family devotions in the home, we'll show you. If you need help talking to your teenager about sex, we'll come alongside you with resources to help you. And if you need an elderly couple to serve as mentors or adopted grandparents for your children, we'll help you find them." To me, this is the role of the church—to be a valuable and necessary partner to families.

Deena and her husband were the parents of two beautiful children, one age nine and the other just a few months old. Deena had been moved by one of my messages regarding the role that parents play in passing on faith to their children. As a result, she made a personal commitment to bring Christ into the center of her life and the life of her family. She called and set up a time to have their youngest child dedicated.

One week before the dedication, Deena called to tell me that her child had died of SIDS. The loss was devastating. I realized how difficult this would be for Deena, so I began to pray for her. Two months later, Deena came to a baptism class that I was leading. When it came time for her to share her personal testimony, the class was blown away! Deena tearfully, yet calmly, shared about the loss of her baby and how devastating it had been for her. But she went on to tell how much more important God had become to her as a result.

Deena said that the church had carried her through the difficult days. She was overwhelmed by the love that the people in the church had showered upon her and her family. She was thankful that she'd gotten to know about God's love for her before this tragedy happened. She knew that God was the source of strength and peace she was experiencing. Now she wanted to be baptized to publicly show that in spite of her pain and unanswered questions, God would continue to be at the center of her life and the life of her family.

On the Sunday Deena was baptized, there wasn't a dry eye in the place! Now, two years later, God has blessed Deena and her husband with another child. Deena has repeatedly said, "I really don't know what I would have done without God and this church. We didn't even know most of these people personally, but they carried us through. They showered us with the love of Christ when we needed it most."

I firmly believe that Christ, through the Church, has something to offer you and your family that you can't find anywhere else. The loving arms of Jesus Christ were able to wrap themselves around Deena and her family in their time of need because they had a relationship with the Bride of Christ, the Church. The truth is that all families will face times when they could use the loving arms of Christ to carry them through their pain or need. That's why Christ gave us the Church—a fellowship of believers who aren't perfect. But through Christ, they become the perfect comforters in our time of crisis.

Third Place

Let's look at how the Bible describes the Church in the Book of Acts. "Every day they continued to meet together in temple courts. They broke bread in their homes and ate together with glad and sincere hearts, praising God and enjoying the favor of all the people" (Acts 2:46-47). I think this example from Scripture shows us the role that the Church should play in the life of every family.

Some people have said that the local church should be your "third place." What does that mean? Each day, you spend the majority of your time in a number of places. The first two places, home and work, establish the foundation for much of your daily routine. Where you eat and sleep and where you make a living tend to do that! But many families battle over identifying and prioritizing what places three, four, five, and so forth should be.

If soccer is your family's third place, you and your family will spend most of your time at soccer fields when you're not at work or home. If school is your family's third place, then school activities will be where you spend most of your time outside of work and home. If the church is your third place, this will define the direction your family will go.

Don't get me wrong—school and extracurricular activities like sports are important when it comes to the growth and development of children. But they simply need to be behind church on the priority scale. Why? Because the Church is the Bride of Christ. God calls us to have a loving relationship with the Church—a love that runs deeper than the love we have for athletics or education. The Early Church described in Acts was a group of people doing life together. They ate together, hung out together, and even sold their goods to help one another out in times of crisis. That's the picture God has for the Church—an intentional Christian community doing life together. And as a result, God continually added to their numbers. I firmly believe that if the Church really started to partner with families and equip them to bring Christ back into the center of the home, we would again see God increase the size and influence of the Church. When families find the help they need, that word will spread like wildfire!

Let's take a look at another text that will help us examine our attitude and behaviors toward the Church.

> Husbands, love your wives, just as Christ loved the church and gave himself up for her to make her holy, cleansing her by the washing with water through the word, and to present her to himself as a radiant church, without stain or wrinkle or any other blemish, but holy and blameless (Eph. 5:25-27).

In these verses, we see Jesus' attitude toward the Church. He clearly loves the Church, and His passion clearly reflects the positive attitude that He maintains toward the Church. Do we have that same positive attitude about the Church?

"Have to" or "Get to"?

When I was a teenager, I didn't enjoy going to church on Sunday mornings. That's putting it mildly. I just wanted to sleep in! Yet every Sunday morning, I woke up to the sound of my mom's voice telling me to "Get up, Mark. Time to go to church."

I'd roll over, hoping it was a bad dream. But my mom persisted. Like a broken record, I'd ask, "Do I have to?" Usually, her response was something to the effect of her adding my middle name, which always meant that I was in trouble. Or she'd ask if she needed to get my dad, which also meant I was in trouble. So I'd reluctantly get out of bed and begin the arduous task of getting ready for church.

One Sunday, my mom surprised me. We went through the routine of "time to get up" and "do I have to?" But this time her reply was different. "No, you don't have to," she said. I couldn't believe my ears! Mom had just said that I didn't have to go to church! Could this be true? Had I finally won the battle? Maybe there was a God after all!

Such were my thoughts for a few fleeting seconds—until she finished her statement, "You don't *have* to go to church. You *get* to go to church!" Perhaps for the first time in my life as a teenager, I didn't have a comeback.

That lesson has stuck with me my entire life. What is my attitude toward my church? Do I have a "have to" attitude or a "get to" attitude? When we truly enter into a relationship with our local church (the Bride of Christ), we should look forward to spending time with her and being in her company. Making her a priority in our life becomes easy, because being with her makes us a stronger family. God gave us the local church as the partner He knew that we'd need to complete our journey through this life. Spending time in the church is something we *get* to do!

Sacrifice

In Ephesians 5:25-27, we also see Jesus' desire to make the Church better. Jesus loves the Church, and His love drove Him to give Himself up for the Church—to cleanse her and make her radiant, holy and blameless.

Do we give ourselves up for the church, or do we expect the church to give herself up for us? Do we come to church saying,

"Thy will be done," or do we come asking the church to accommodate "my will being done"?

We live in a world where everything is focused on meeting our individual needs. The "My way right away at Burger King now" slogan or the popular "It's all about me" T-shirts are perfect examples of this reality. To be honest, I see the same attitude every Sunday morning when people critically assess the music, the message and the programs that our church offers, or even the way I dress. Instead of pouring themselves into their church community, many people sit back looking for a reason to criticize the church and leave it.

> As families, we need to become active in the ministries of the church, build relationships with the people and use our gifts to serve the Body. When we do this, we'll be blessed.

Of course, the Church isn't perfect. It's earned some of the criticism it's received. If you look at anything long enough, you'll find a good reason to be critical. But it's also important to remember that the Church was not perfect when Jesus loved her and poured Himself into her!

As families, we need to pour ourselves into the church. We need to become active in the ministries, build relationships with the people and use our gifts to serve the Body. When we do this, we'll be blessed. We can't sit just on the sidelines or only come on Christmas and Easter and expect that to be enough to help us as a family.

Jesus states in Matthew 5:6, "Blessed are those who hunger and thirst for righteousness, for they will be [satisfied]." Are you hungry and thirsty as a family to be blessed and satisfied by God? Then you need to learn how to live a righteous life. You do this by immersing yourself in the right kind of community—the

Christian church, where the people are learning together how to live a "right" kind of life.

A pastor friend of mine recently shared with me, "The degree to which you hunger and thirst for righteousness is the degree to which you'll be satisfied." I don't believe that you can really know God or sustain a relationship with Him without being actively connected to and with a body of believers who are hungering and thirsting to live life God's way. The degree to which you actively engage yourself in the life of an intentional Christian community is the degree to which you'll be satisfied as a family.

After 15 years in ministry working face-to-face with families, I've seen some families commit to making the church the third place in their lives while other families have tried to continually negotiate what that third place is. What I have seen is that those who clearly make the church the third place in their lives find their family life is much more satisfying and fulfilling. This doesn't mean that life is easier for them—they face the same trials that all families face. Yet their faith is able to carry them through because it's more deeply established and ingrained in their lives. Many of these families had tried to live life apart from the Church, but they quickly discovered that life apart from the Bride of Christ was much more difficult than life with the Bride of Christ.

I like the story of the man who became frustrated with his local church and decided to leave. When a new pastor came to town, he visited the man at his home. When the pastor introduced himself, the man quickly responded, "Pastor, I know why you're here, so let me cut to the chase. I'm not coming back to church, no matter what you say. That place is filled with a bunch of hypocrites, and I don't want anything to do with them."

The pastor calmly replied, "That's fine, but could I come in and have a cup of coffee with you?" The man opened the door and the pastor entered and took a seat in the living room next to the fireplace. The pastor grabbed the tongs and reached into the fire that was burning and pulled out a log. He placed the log in front of the fire away from the other burning logs and then sat down to drink his coffee. Both men stared at the log and watched as it went from being burning hot to a quickly dying and smoking ember.

After the pastor had finished his cup of coffee, he got up again, went over to the log—which was now almost completely out—picked it up with the tongs, and placed it back into the fire. Quickly, the log became engulfed in flames again. The pastor turned to the man and said, "Thanks for the coffee," and then left.

The next Sunday, the man was back in church again. He realized that apart from the church, the flame of his relationship with God would weaken over time and eventually die out.

The Journey Through Life

It's not easy being a family today. Satan takes delight in tearing families apart, because he knows the pain and devastation it causes. It's also not easy being a Christian, because sin and temptation surround us at every turn. Given this, it's pretty safe to conclude that being a Christian family is doubly difficult. And that's precisely the reason why the church is so important. As Christian families, we need a place where we can laugh together and cry together—a place where we can grow together and learn from one another as we take this journey through life.

I'll never forget Justin. He was a sharp teenager, but unfortunately he had an addictive personality. As an eighth grader, he became involved in drugs, and that's when the roller-coaster ride began. Over the next two years, there were periods of time when Justin was clean, followed by periods of time when he was using again. Through it all, our church remained committed to him and his family.

In high school, Justin's addiction became so severe that he got into trouble with the law. Eventually, he found himself in a forced treatment program. To further complicate things, while Justin was in this 12-month treatment facility, his parents went through a divorce. As his pastor, I was allowed to visit Justin every other week, and during one of my visits, Justin asked for a Bible. Our church continued to support Jordan and both of his parents. When Justin was finally released from the treatment program, he and his mom moved to Canada. I presumed that would be the last that I would ever see of him.

Three years later, I was serving in another congregation. As I greeted people after the service, to my surprise, there stood Justin. He was now a grown man with a pregnant woman standing next to him. He introduced me to his wife, and then we went out to lunch. During lunch, he made a comment that I will never forget. He said, "Mark, I could never thank you enough for the way the church stood by me during my drug addiction. You never judged me or gave up on me, even after I'd given up on myself. I came to see you because I've been clean for over three years, and I wanted to say thank you. I couldn't have done it without you or the church."

All that was enough to put me on the brink of tears. But then Justin continued and said, "By the way, we're wondering if you would be the godparent for our baby?" That did it—the tears flowed!

I could fill these pages with stories of people like Deena or Justin who've said, "I don't know how I would have survived without the church." Although the church is far from perfect— and sadly, many of these imperfections make the news—I have regularly seen how God perfects the church in our time of need. That's why I believe the church can be the family's best friend, if only we would enter into a committed relationship with her.

Finding the Right Church

In addition to working with parents and families, I've had the opportunity to work with hundreds of congregations all around the world. My calling has been to help them understand how they can do a better job of equipping the home to be the primary place where faith is nurtured.

I'd like to tell you that all Christian churches are committed to this goal. But regrettably, this isn't true. Some churches still enable and even encourage the "drop off your kids" mentality. In these churches, if you're not there to volunteer, they'd prefer you to just stay away so that they can teach your children the faith.

It's extremely important that you find the right "partner" for your family. As you explore finding the right church for you and your family, here are the types of questions that I suggest you ask:

- What is the senior pastor's view of the relationship between church and home?
- Is passing on faith to children through a partnership with parents a part of the mission and values of the church?
- How will the church partner with and equip you to pass on the faith to your children?
- Matthew 6:21 says, "Where your treasure is, there your heart will be also." What percentage of the church budget is committed to children and to youth and family ministry?
- Are the children's, youth and family ministries growing?
- Can the church introduce you to some families whose lives have been changed as a result of their involvement with the church?

And finally, let me give you three final suggestions when looking for the right church.

1. *Pray for God to lead you to the right church.* He has the right church in mind for you, and He will show you which one it is.
2. *Take your time.* You don't need to hurry. Look at a few churches before making your decision. In most cases, this will confirm which church is the right one for you.
3. *When God leads you to the right church, make a full commitment to it.* Remember, the Church is the Bride of Christ! Treat your commitment like a sacred marriage vow. Stay committed in good times and in bad, in sickness and in health, till death do you part! Don't "church hop." Get rid of the attitude that says, "If the church does what I like, how I like it, then I'll stay. But if it doesn't, I'm out of here!" In the Bible's descriptions of the Early Church, some of the greatest growth occurred when it experienced trials and troubles. If you prayerfully arrive at the decision that God has led you to a specific church, then trust that God will grow you and your family in and through that church.

Full Circle

Well, we've now come full circle. In the Introduction, we acknowledged that all families are dysfunctional and in need of a makeover. In chapter 1, we recognized that this family makeover begins in the home, so that it can once again become the primary place where faith is nurtured. In chapter 2, we learned that parents are called to be the "bishops, apostles and priests" of their own homes, and that we can't abdicate this responsibility to others. In chapter 3, we looked at the critical role that faith plays in the lives of our children, and we discussed how to pass on our faith to them by talking about it when we lie down and when we get up. In chapter 4, we rediscovered the importance that grandparents and other elders can play in helping to pass on our Christian faith to our children and children's children. Finally, in chapter 5, we've seen that the church's role is to come alongside the family, equipping them to pass on faith in the home.

So let me close this book where I began. I believe that the home is the primary place where faith is to be nurtured. If our families are going to be able to stand up to Satan's attacks, we must have Christ in the center of each and every one of our homes. This begins with the love of Christ in our hearts as parents. It then becomes firmly established in each child as our lifestyle reflects that we're walking with Christ 24 hours a day, 7 days a week. This lifestyle won't be easy, but that's why God gave us the Church—an intentional Christian community filled with elders and fellow sojourners—to serve as a resource and safe haven for our families.

That's it! I believe this is what every family needs to succeed!

Notes

1. George Barna, *Transforming Children Into Spiritual Champions* (Ventura, CA: Regal Books), pp. 83-84.
2. Ibid., pp. 93-94.

Church Makeover Keys

Key 1: God didn't intend the local church to be a drop-off center for your children.

Key 2: Satan wants to keep you from becoming part of the church because he knows it can help you and your family.

Key 3: Not all churches are the same. You need to find a church that will equip you and your home to be the primary place where your family's faith is nurtured.

Key 4: When you find the right church, you need to commit to it wholeheartedly. It needs to become your family's "third place."

Family Activities

ACTIVITY 1
Car Time Notes

When I was growing up, our youth pastor had us turn in sermon notes each week. He wanted us to be worshiping on a consistent basis, so he required us to turn in three sets of sermon notes each month.

This wasn't all that complicated. He had the members of our youth group answer the same three questions each time:

1. What was the key Bible verse in today's message?
2. What is one lesson you learned?
3. What difference is this going to make in your life?

Write down these three questions and keep them in your car. Feel free to adapt them as needed, but keep the questions simple. Each week after church, take turns answering these questions on the ride home.

FAMILY ACTIVITY 2
My Family's Spiritual Gifts

God gives each Christian spiritual gifts. His gifts have a single purpose: to build up the body of believers. The gifts of the Spirit are special abilities, or traits, that God gives to the believers that enable us to do many wonderful things for Him.

Where do we first learn about ourselves? The family is the place where we start discovering who we are. Where do we first try things out? We try things out with our parents, siblings, grandparents, aunts and uncles. Who cheers us on and picks us up after the first wobbly attempts? Our family members love us and surround us with support. These are the day-to-day realities of our lives. So what better place than our family to start learning about our spiritual gifts and how to use them in service to God and others.

How old do you need to be for this activity? I realized that my daughter had the gift of administration when she was less than a year old. When we put a newspaper next to her, she'd sort it page by page and put the entire paper on her left. Then she'd sort it again and move it page by page to the right. She was an organizer from the very beginning (and this activity kept her busy for hours!). So I believe that you can begin to see spiritual gifts in your children at a very early age. (You may want to do this activity again in a year or two to see if God has brought any unused gift to the forefront.)

Get started by making copies of the following page(s) for each member of your family. Then, individually, complete the following steps:

1. Go through the spiritual gifts that are listed and check the gifts you think you have. What gifts do you bring to the family?

2. List your family members (parents, children, grand-parents and so on) and then go through the spiritual gifts again and check the gifts you think each individual family member has.

3. Have each family member complete steps 1 and 2.

Then, as a family, complete these steps:

1. Share what you discovered with each other. Is there unanimous agreement on some of the gifts—in other words, everyone agrees that a certain person has a certain gift? Is there disagreement regarding a particular gift?

2. What gifts do all of your family members share in common?

3. Discuss how the members of your family can collectively use their gifts to serve Christ.

Chart 5

	YOU	NAME	NAME	NAME

Gifts of Action

Administration—This person is able to understand and set goals for various groups. This person is able to plan, organize and get things done.

Craftsmanship—This person can use his/her hands to build things.

Arts and Crafts—This person can use his/her hands in creative and artistic ways.

Encouragement—This person has the ability to give words of comfort, support to people in a way that helps them.

Leadership—This person has the ability to motivate and direct people to get things done.

Music-Vocal—The ability to sing joyfully. The next American Idol!

Music-Instrumental—The ability to joyfully play an instrument.

Gifts of the Heart

Faith—The ability to have confidence in God in all circumstances.

Giving—The enjoyment of sharing your resources to help others.

Hospitality—The joy of welcoming people into your home and serving them.

Mercy—The ability to care for those who are hurting or in need.

Serving—The ability to identify and meet needs in the community or world.

Gifts of Inspiration

Prayer—The enjoyment of praying frequently and specifically for others.

Chart 5 continued

	YOU	NAME	NAME	NAME
Teaching—The ability to explain things to others in a way they can understand.	___	___	___	___
Wisdom—The ability to offer sound advice.	___	___	___	___
Writing—The ability to put your thoughts and ideas into meaningful words that influence others.	___	___	___	___

Gifts of Proclamation

Discernment—The ability to know right from wrong, good and evil, truth and error.	___	___	___	___
Evangelism—The ability and passion to easily tell others about Jesus.	___	___	___	___
Knowledge—The ability to discover new truths, ideas and information.	___	___	___	___

Small-Group Discussion Starters

1. After work and home, what are the next three priorities in your life? How has that changed through the years?
2. What role did the church play in your childhood?
3. How did you arrive at the church that you currently attend? What other church experiences have you had?
4. As you reflect on this entire book, what was the most important point that you'll remember? What was the best practical idea or activity you'll use?

More Resources by Mark Holmen

Take It Home
Inspiration and Events to
Help Parents Spiritually Transform
Their Children
Mark Holmen and *Dave Teixeira*
ISBN 978.08307.44572

Building Faith at Home
Why Faith at Home Must Be
Your Church's #1 Priority
Mark Holmen
ISBN 978.08307.45029